高校英语选修课系列教材

# 英语报刊选读教程

## 第三版

胡 阳 编著

清华大学出版社
北京

## 内 容 简 介

本书是在2010年第二版教材的基础上修订而成。新版教材在沿用原有编写理念的同时在文章选材、板块设计、练习编排等方面进行了修订。本书按主题分为8个单元，每单元包括1篇新闻、3篇文章。所选文章渐进地增加阅读长度和难度，其后附上一定的阅读理解和词汇练习，以及适量的写作练习，适合大中专院校中已完成英语初级阶段学习的非英语专业学习者使用，所选阅读文章均来自近年来原版英文报刊杂志，题材多样。此外，为方便使用，本书附有练习答案。

本书同样适合大中专院校中水平较高的英语学习者和大学英语四六级、研究生入学考试及TOFEL、GRE等各类考生备考使用。

版权所有，侵权必究。侵权举报电话：010-62782989，beiqinquan@tup.tsinghua.edu.cn。

图书在版编目（CIP）数据

英语报刊选读教程 / 胡阳编著.—3版.—北京：清华大学出版社，2018（2024.1重印）
（高校英语选修课系列教材）
ISBN 978-7-302-49705-9

Ⅰ.①英… Ⅱ.①胡… Ⅲ.①英语-阅读教学-高等学校-教材 Ⅳ.①H319.37

中国版本图书馆CIP数据核字（2018）第035647号

责任编辑：徐　静
封面设计：子　一
责任校对：王凤芝
责任印制：丛怀宇

出版发行：清华大学出版社
网　　址：https://www.tup.com.cn, https://www.wqxuetang.com
地　　址：北京清华大学学研大厦A座　　邮　编：100084
社 总 机：010-83470000　　邮　购：010-62786544
投稿与读者服务：010-62776969, c-service@tup.tsinghua.edu.cn
质量反馈：010-62772015, zhiliang@tup.tsinghua.edu.cn

印 装 者：三河市少明印务有限公司
经　　销：全国新华书店
开　　本：185mm×260mm　　印　张：16.5　　字　数：314千字
版　　次：2003年7月第1版　2018年8月第3版　　印　次：2024年1月第5次印刷
定　　价：68.00元

产品编号：068617-03

# 第三版说明

《英语报刊选读教程》首版于 2003 年，2010 年修订出版第二版。

报刊文章（包括纸媒与网络）有其明显的时效性，瞬息万变的世界形势必然带来思维及语言的变化，为保证语言学习者的英语学习及知识结构与时俱进，故选编第三版。

第三版在课文编排及练习设计上仍保持前两版的教学理念与基本格局，但在以下几方面做了修订：

1. 文章内容方面，更换了所有新闻文章及三分之二的课文，以保持其时效性强的特点。

2. 单元设计方面，调整了主题顺序，第六单元的主题 Society 改为 Global Development，以期更好地反映世界发展的正能量现象。

3. 板块设计方面，每篇文章的课后练习都增加了 From Reading to Writing/Speaking，增加基于输入的输出训练，以提高学生的语言应用能力，同时也为整体语言技能训练提供更多可能。本练习的设计理念为训练学生真正的日常及学术交际能力（口头与书面），包括信息描述、摘要写作、观点陈述，以及有效提问等能力。

编 者

2017 年 12 月于清华园

# 第二版说明

《英语报刊选读教程》首版于 2003 年，为全国多所高校使用，并受到广大英语学习者的欢迎。

报刊文章有其明显的时效性，首版教材出版至今已逾 7 载，期间国际、国内形势发生了巨大变化，英语语言的使用自然也随之发生变化。为保证英语学习者的英语学习也与时俱进，及时了解国内外社会变化与发展，接触新鲜的语言语料，故选编第二版。

第二版在课文编排和练习设计上仍保持首版的格局，沿用首版的编写理念，但在以下几方面做了修订：

1. 单元设计方面，把原有的 War 和 Government 两单元归为一个单元：Politics，增加了一个单元：Disasters，使学习内容更适合大学英语学习者，同时也更好地反映了近两年的热点话题。

2. 文章内容方面，更换了部分课文，以保证内容信息的时代性，且所选文章长度及难易度更合适；同时，更强调文章内容的积极向上，如一些诺贝尔获奖者的成就及对人类的贡献、奥林匹克精神等，以起到教书育人的作用。

3. 板块设计方面，每个单元开始增加了新闻阅读，以及按照新闻五要素设计的问题。一方面，这可以增加内容题材的多样性、趣味性。另一方面，这些新闻可以为教学活动提供更多的素材，如教师可用它们做口语练习（用问答形式），使学生的口语水平提高一个层次，从日常对话到有能力谈论时事。

4. 为加强语言方面的学习，每篇文章后增加了 Useful Expressions 部分，列出了相关文章中的主要短语或表达方式，以方便学生掌握语言点。同时 Notes 部分讲解更为详尽。

编　者

2010 年 4 月于清华园

# 第一版前言

我们在教学中发现,很多学生由于语言水平的局限,习惯于逐字逐句地阅读,注意力通常集中在字和句上,尤其是那些自己不认识的词上。这也就是为什么多数外语学习者总觉得词汇量太小,读不懂,不知作者(文章)所云。那么如何才能成为一个熟练的外语阅读者呢?首先要克服一些不良的阅读习惯,养成良好的阅读习惯,如:

1. 用手、尺子、铅笔等指着单词,一个字一个字地读,这样无形中降低了阅读速度。要养成按照"意群"阅读的习惯,放宽眼睛"扫描"的范围,以提高阅读速度。这可以通过摘抄"好词佳句"来练习。本书每篇文章后的 Useful Expressions 部分就是一个示范。记忆也要从单纯的单词记忆转为短语、句子记忆。

2. 必须读出声才能理解。也就是说,首先要把字符变成声音,然后由声音转化成意义,这实际上多了一个阅读程序,速度自然也就慢了下来。出声阅读是阅读的初级阶段,要成为一个熟练的阅读者,必须有意识地多进行"默读"练习,学会将字符直接转化成意义的技能。

3. 只动眼睛不动手,这是许多学习者总觉得记不住文章内容的原因之一。阅读时一定要手眼并用,学会做批注,即边阅读,边把标志文章脉络的重点信息或重点词语画出来,这一方面帮助记忆,另一方面也帮助理解。

4. 遇到生词就画下来,这是为什么许多英语学习者总觉得生词太多读不懂的原因之一。通常在阅读时用笔画下的应该是文章的重点,这一点我们回忆一下阅读汉语文章的过程就能发现。而遇到生词就画下来实际上对理解文章毫无帮助,而且会给阅读者本人造成一种心理压力(这么多生词肯定读不懂!),尤其在考试时就更是如此。那么试着把注意力集中到那些已经认识的词或短语上来，你会发现根据这些即使你不能理解所有的细节，也能够理解文章的基本思想。

现在我们来了解一下阅读过程。其实，外语阅读和母语阅读一样，都是为了了解文章的中心议题，获取信息。具体的阅读过程应该是：希望获得的信息（expectation）→了解中心思想→了解有关主题的不同观点→了解作者所持观点→作者如何论述（证实）自己的观点（也就是说，作者是如何说服读者的）。那么要完成这一过程，读者的注意力就应该集中在句间关系、段落与段落之间的关系上。

**提问式阅读法**

我们知道任何文章都是为了传达某种信息，而篇章的每一句话，甚至一个词都是为传达某种信息服务的，前后句子与段落通常有相互说明、解释的逻辑关系。本书介绍的"提问式阅读法"可使这种逻辑关系明朗化，在很大程度上解决了因语言水平有限带来的阅读困难，帮助提高阅读速度与效率。

一般来说，每篇文章，甚至每句话，都有可能包含六个方面的信息：who、what、where、when、why、how。根据"提问式阅读法"，首先，读者在读文章标题时，就标题关键词进行这六个方面的信息提问，然后到文章中去寻找所提问题的答案，这些答案实际上就是文章的中心思想。然后，在阅读过程中，每读一句话，读者可就其中不定因素或自己想了解的信息提问，然后在下文中去寻找答案。通常下一句话，或下一段落就可解决所提问题。这样，读者在阅读过程中是主动与作者展开对话，主动索取信息。使用这种方法阅读就会越读越明白，而不是只懂"只言片语"，所谓"只见树木，不见森林"。

**本书的特色及编写目的**

本书的主要编写目的是使学生了解英文报纸杂志各种体裁文章的语言特点，帮助其学会如何快速有效地从所读文章中获得最大限度的信息，以训练学生主动索取信息的习惯和能力，从而提高学生阅读能力。与国内外已出版的同类书相比，特色在于：

（1）目的明确：文章编排及练习设计围绕"训练学生主动索取信息的习惯和能力"这一主要目的，而非"包罗万象"。

（2）方法独特：从句间关系入手，探索"问答式"（问题—解决）阅读方法，提高学生主动阅读和准确理解语言的能力，训练其快速获取信息的能力。

（3）信息量大：本书所选8个主题及其文章与生活和社会紧密结合，使学生在提高阅读能力的同时，丰富其科学、文化、经济等方面的背景知识，了解时事，扩大其知识面。

（4）时代性强：所有文章选自近两年原版英文报纸杂志，同时考虑内容的持久性和语言的典型性。

（5）实践性强：学生在进行大量阅读后可进行写作、讨论和口头报告等活动。

（6）方便好用：本书编排简洁明了，练习指示及讲解语言简单易懂。

## 本书的编排设计及使用

本书的编排与设计基于上述基本思想，各种问题贯穿始终，包括如下六个部分：

（1）每个单元以一篇同主题的 News Reading 开始，配以按照新闻报道特点（5W）的问题。

（2）每个单元的第1篇文章设计有 Pre-reading Questions 放在文章标题下面，同时要求学生自己就文章标题提问，然后到文章中去寻找答案。对于找不到答案的问题，可要求学生自己查阅相关文章阅读。这一练习将潜意识的母语阅读习惯有意识化，从而帮助提高学生主动阅读的能力。（见 Reading Strategy, Unit 1）

（3）每单元前两篇文章配有 Margin Questions，放在相应行的页边空白处，以训练学生在阅读过程中主动索取信息的习惯和能力，书后所附答案告知在何处可找到答案，以帮助学生了解句子与句子、段落与段落之间的关系。其中 QUESTIONS：_____? 要求学生自己就相应行的句子提问。建议教师在授课过程中坚持以上两种问题的练习，以帮助学生养成为了掌握信息而非单词而阅读（read for information, not for words）的习惯。每单元第3篇文章可以要求学生自己给出 Pre-reading 和 Margin 问题。（见 Reading Strategy, Unit Two & Three）

（4）课后阅读理解练习包含主观、客观两种类型，检查学生对所读文章事实、主题大意等的理解程度，同时可以训练学生应试能力。

（5）词汇练习则着重训练学生根据上下文确定含义的能力，练习分主观、客观两种，包括常用词和生词的词义确定，和文章细节的确定。短语练习目的在于引起学生对固定搭配、句子结构等的重视，为使用地道的英语做准备。（见

Reading Strategy, Unit Four & Eight）

（6）每个单元结尾处设计有Assignments，要求学生对所读文章的观点和信息进行评论，并表述自己的观点，目的在于训练学生清楚表达自己的观点或阅读体会，学会思考，学会用英语与他人交流观点和体会。Assignments要求学生列出读完文章后仍遗留的问题，即在所读文章中没有找到答案的问题，目的是鼓励学生自己进一步阅读其他相关文章，以扩大其阅读量，提高其主动阅读的兴趣。

以上六个部分包含所在文章的所有语言点，一方面帮助准确理解文章内容及作者观点，另一方面帮助英语学习者掌握良好的阅读方法，训练其良好的阅读习惯，学会如何快速有效地从所读文章中获得最大限度的信息，以训练学生主动索取信息的习惯和能力，从而提高其阅读能力。

感谢清华大学出版社鼎力相助。本书受清华大学校级规划教材建设资助，特此致谢。

恳请读者朋友及各位同仁对本书不当与不足之处进行批评指正。

编　者

2002年12月6日于清华园

# Contents

| | | |
|---|---|---|
| **Unit 1** | **Education** | ..................................................1 |
| **Part A** | **Lead-in** | ......................................................2 |
| News Reading | Schoolchildren Fearful about Future since EU Referendum, Say Heads | ..................................2 |
| **Part B** | **Reading** | ......................................................4 |
| Reading 1 | Will Online Learning Replace the Classroom? | ......................4 |
| Reading 2 | No Grades, No Timetable: Berlin School Turns Teaching Upside Down | ..................................15 |
| Reading 3 | "Hire" Education: A Vocational Model Succeeds | ..................22 |
| **Part C** | **Unit Assignments** | ........................................28 |

| | | |
|---|---|---|
| **Unit 2** | **Science and Technology** | ......................29 |
| **Part A** | **Lead-in** | ....................................................30 |
| News Reading | Go Humans: Lee Sedol Scores First Victory Against Supercomputer | ..................................30 |
| **Part B** | **Reading** | ....................................................33 |
| Reading 1 | Navigate the Jungle of Tech Ecosystems | ...................33 |
| Reading 2 | The Robots Are Coming | ..........................................43 |
| Reading 3 | The Simple, Free Solution to Asia's Myopia Epidemic | ...........51 |
| **Part C** | **Unit Assignments** | ........................................57 |

| | | |
|---|---|---|
| **Unit 3** | **Disasters** | ..................................................59 |
| **Part A** | **Lead-in** | ....................................................60 |
| News Reading | Yangtze Basin Hit by Flooding with Storms Spanning 1,000 Miles | ..................................................60 |
| **Part B** | **Reading** | ....................................................62 |
| Reading 1 | Different Natural Disasters, Same Risky Human Habits | ................62 |

| | | |
|---|---|---|
| Reading 2 | Midwest Floods Leave Red Cross in the Red | 70 |
| Reading 3 | Humans Add to Natural Disaster Risk | 76 |
| **Part C** | **Unit Assignments** | **82** |

## Unit 4  Sports .......................................................... 83

| | | |
|---|---|---|
| **Part A** | **Lead-in** | **84** |
| News Reading | Li Jianrou Wins 500m Gold | 84 |
| **Part B** | **Reading** | **88** |
| Reading 1 | Brexit Wins: How Will British Sport Be Affected? | 88 |
| Reading 2 | Education the Heart of Olympics Says Rogge | 99 |
| Reading 3 | Grudge Match | 105 |
| **Part C** | **Unit Assignments** | **112** |

## Unit 5  Global Development ........................ 113

| | | |
|---|---|---|
| **Part A** | **Lead-in** | **114** |
| News Reading | World Health Organisation Reports Dramatic Fall in Malaria Deaths | 114 |
| **Part B** | **Reading** | **117** |
| Reading 1 | Who Owns You? | 117 |
| Reading 2 | The Feelgood Factor | 126 |
| Reading 3 | Woman Challenges Tradition, Brings Change to Her Kenyan Village | 132 |
| **Part C** | **Unit Assignments** | **139** |

## Unit 6  Environment ..................................... 141

| | | |
|---|---|---|
| **Part A** | **Lead-in** | **142** |
| News Reading | Climate Protesters Invade UK's Largest Opencast Coalmine | 142 |

| | | |
|---|---|---|
| **Part B** | **Reading** | **145** |
| Reading 1 | How Do You Junk Your Computer | 145 |
| Reading 2 | Climate Change Lights the Touchpaper on Terror—We Must Fight Them Together | 156 |
| Reading 3 | A Tree Grows in Kenya | 164 |
| **Part C** | **Unit Assignments** | **170** |

# Unit 7 Politics .................................................. 171

| | | |
|---|---|---|
| **Part A** | **Lead-in** | **172** |
| News Reading | UK Must Be Involved in EU Anti-terrorism Measures, Says Keith Vaz | 172 |
| **Part B** | **Reading** | **175** |
| Reading 1 | Win-win Governance | 175 |
| Reading 2 | The New Words of War | 184 |
| Reading 3 | Progress Against Corruption | 191 |
| **Part C** | **Unit Assignments** | **197** |

# Unit 8 Economics .............................................. 199

| | | |
|---|---|---|
| **Part A** | **Lead-in** | **200** |
| News Reading | Tax Havens Have No Economic Justification, Say Top Economists | 200 |
| **Part B** | **Reading** | **204** |
| Reading 1 | The Problem with Profits | 204 |
| Reading 2 | Evaluating Good Corporate Citizenship | 215 |
| Reading 3 | "Banker" Who Lends to the Poor Wins Nobel Peace Prize | 221 |
| **Part C** | **Unit Assignments** | **226** |

# Key to the Exercises ............................................ 227

# Unit 1

# Education

# Part A
# Lead-in

## Schoolchildren Fearful about Future since EU Referendum, Say Heads[1]

Teaching union calls on David Cameron to reassure pupils from elsewhere in EU they will not be forced to leave Britain.

*By Richard Adams*

[1] A leading head teachers' union has asked the prime minister for reassurances about the status of schoolchildren from other EU countries enrolled in British schools, after last week's vote to leave the European Union.

[2] The National Association of Head Teachers (NAHT) has urged David Cameron to make a statement addressing EU pupils' fears about their future status.

[3] A letter signed by the union's general secretary, Russell Hobby, says, "School leaders are reporting to us that some of their young students are worrying about their future."

[4] "Pupils are worried about being forced to leave Britain. They are fearful of

---

1. Adopted from *The Guardian*, Jun. 30, 2016

a potential rise in racism and community conflict. They are concerned about their prospects in an uncertain and isolated Britain."

[5] "It is not just the economic markets that need calming. Our young people need a statement from the government to address their fears."

[6] "NAHT strongly urges the government to give pupils from the EU better assurance that they will be able to complete their school education without interruption; that they and their families remain welcome and valued members of the communities they call home."

[7] A spokesperson for the Department for Education responded, "No child should live in fear of racism or bullying. The prime minister has been clear there will be no immediate changes for European citizens living in the UK. We will not stand for intolerance and hate crimes of any kind must be stamped out."

[8] Cameron said yesterday that it would be up to any future prime minister to decide the status of EU nationals living in Britain.

[9] The prime minister added that there were no plans to change their residency rights before negotiations to leave the EU had been completed.

 **Answer the following questions.**

1. Why are schoolchildren fearful about their future?

2. What kind of schoolchildren are fearful about their future?

3. What was the EU referendum?

4. What should be done to address their fears?

5. What were the responses from the British government to the children's fear?

# Part B
## Reading

# Will Online Learning Replace the Classroom?[1]

*By Avi Yashchin*

**Pre-reading Questions**

1. What is online learning?

2. What kind of online courses have you ever taken?

3. Do you like online learning? Why?

4. What advantages or disadvantages does online learning have?

*Your questions before reading the article:*

1. _____

2. _____

3. _____

4. _____

5. _____

---

1. Adopted from *The Huff Post*, Nov. 3, 2014

# Unit 1  Education

> Words you know related to this topic:
> 
> __school__  _____  _____  _____
> _____  _____  _____  _____
> _____  _____  _____  _____

[1] In a time when most American toddlers are as comfortable with a touchscreen as with a crayon, one would be remiss to think that the current classroom-based model of education will survive as is. Change is most evident in higher education, where massive open online courses (MOOCs) account for a growing share of academic content, but exactly how much disruption can we expect from online learning?

1. Why is it remiss to think that?
2. What change?
3. Then how much?

[2] Web-based education technology has seen both promising and lackluster results in terms of adoption and course completion rates; however, online education proponents assure us that the traditional classroom is on the cusp of a dramatic change.

4. What is promising?
5. What is lackluster?
6. Why should traditional classroom change?

[3] The imminent IPO of 2U, an online education company that partners with colleges and universities, is a vote of confidence for the ed tech space. Filing to raise up to $100 million, 2U's primary underwriters include Goldman Sachs and Credit Suisse. 2U already partners with such reputable institutions as Berkeley, USC, Georgetown and American University, remotely offering "online learning experiences that match or exceed the quality and rigor found on campus".

7. Why do these institutions support online learning?

## The Benefits of Online Learning

[4] Internet-based platforms have empowered us to replace or remotely facilitate many historically

8. What are the benefits of online learning?

interactive processes—like shopping, dating and banking. Attaining an education might be the next frontier for web-based expediency, and there's a host of reasons why:

• **Affordability:** Over 300 lecture hours at Berkeley, Harvard and MIT are available, for free, on YouTube. MOOCs are designed to be free for participants and open to anyone, and other online learning platforms are made inexpensive for the end user. The online medium is scalable because of its reduced overhead compared with brick-and-mortar schools.

• **Convenience:** Allowing students to take courses on their own time, at their own pace, online learning systems are far more convenient than their in-person counterparts. Forums and online communities built around courses add to the usability of these distance education programs.

• **Accessibility:** For-profit colleges were early adopters of online learning, since it allowed them to attract customers who were otherwise unlikely to attend any sort of higher education. MOOCs and other online classes attract and retain a diverse mix of student backgrounds, geographies, experiences and motivations.

• **Customizability:** Online education affords students greater flexibility to choose when, where, what, how and how much they learn. "Learners are in control," said Andrew Ho of Harvard's Graduate School of Education after an analysis of working papers on Harvard and MIT's joint EdX program, involving

9. What will be the next project for the Internet-based platform?
10. What are the reasons?
11. What is the affordability?

12. What is the convenience?

13. What are accessible?
14. To whom is it accessible?

15. What can be customized?

841,687 registrants in 17 open online courses. Students were found to have varied reasons for taking EdX MOOCs; some were just hoping to learn, some were looking for resources to aid in other classes they were taking, and others were teachers seeking insights on how to teach their own classes.

• **Preparation:** Future employers will prefer job candidates who are familiar with dynamic learning, says Thunderbird Online. It is a self-serving assertion coming from the online education provider, no doubt, but if we consider the fact that online learning is increasingly implemented as a training tool in corporations, the argument might already ring true.

[5] In their book, Disrupting Class: How Disruptive Innovation Will Change the Way the World Learns, co-authors Clayton Christensen and Michael Horn argue that America's lack of innovation in the classroom is to blame for this nation's students' underperformance in comparison with other countries' students. The fix? Customized learning through technological innovation.

## A Long Way to Go, According to the Numbers

[6] In 2012, more than 6.7 million students took at least one online course, representing an all-time high of 32 percent of higher education students. The Babson Study, which assembled these data, reports that this 9.3 percent year-over-year enrollment growth rate is the lowest in the history of the 10-year series, but it's still higher than the overall enrollment rate in higher education.

16. What preparation?

17. What is the assertion?

18. What argument?

19. The fix to what?
20. And how is the innovation going?

21. How is the enrollment of online education?

[7] Despite a record high in online enrollment, the EdX analysis conducted by MIT and Harvard revealed some surprising attrition rates. Of the learners in the study, 95 percent of students dropped their online class before getting a completion certificate. But researchers Andrew Ho and Isaac Chuang say these low completion rates are not cause for concern; indeed they are a misleading metric. Ho said, "A better criterion for success might be for students to complete more of the course than they thought they would, or to learn more than they might have expected." More productive key takeaways were the diversity of registrants, the apparent interest of non-traditional learners, and the innovation that results from this type of experimentation.

[8] The Babson Research Study revealed that academic leaders are undecided about MOOCs as a sustainable method for offering courses, with most (45.2 percent) being neutral, and the remainder evenly split between the two opposing opinions. Less than three percent of higher education institutions currently offer a MOOC. While 69.1 percent of chief academic officers claim that online learning represents a critical part of their long-term strategy, only 9.4 percent are in the planning stages of implementing a MOOC, suggesting that other types of online education are expected to emerge in colleges and universities.

22. What are the surprising attrition rates?

23. Why needn't we worry about the low completion rates?

24. Whose takeaways are they?

25. Why are they undecided?

26. What are the opposing opinions?

Unit 1　Education

 **Useful Expressions**

| | |
|---|---|
| on the cusp of a dramatic change | 处于重大变革的关口 |
| partner with | 与……合作 |
| a vote of confidence for... | 对……有信心 |
| ed tech space | 教育科技空间 |
| end user | 终端使用者 |
| ring true | 听上去是真实的 |
| attrition rates | 退学率 |

 **Notes**

1. In a time when most American toddlers are as comfortable with a touchscreen as with a crayon, one would be remiss to think that the current classroom-based model of education will survive as is. (Para.1) 在多数美国学步的孩子都能像拿彩笔一样熟练使用触屏的时代，如果人们依旧认为现在的教室教育模式仍然会继续就太大意了。
本句的介词短语为时间状语，它同时包含一个由 when 引导的时间状语从句；主句包含一个 that 引导的宾语从句。as is 照原样

2. IPO (Para.3) 首次公开募股 (Initial Public Offerings，简称 IPO)

3. Filing to raise up to $100 million, 2U's primary underwriters include Goldman Sachs and Credit Suisse. (Para.3) 在把价格提升到一亿美元后，2U 的两个基本承购人包括高盛公司和瑞信银行。
本句中，现在分词短语做时间状语。

4. 2U already partners with such reputable institutions as Berkeley, USC, Georgetown and American University, remotely offering "online learning experiences that match or exceed the quality and rigor found on campus". (Para.3) 2U 已经和一些有声望的机构合作了，如伯克利、南加州大学 (USC)、乔治敦大学和美国大学，远程提供"网络学习经验以符合乃至超越已经建立起来的校园品质及严谨"。

本句中，现在分词短语做结果状语。

5. The online medium is scalable because of its reduced overhead compared with brick-and-mortar schools. (Para.4) 与实体学校相比，网络课堂因管理费的减少而较易伸缩。

6. Forums and online communities built around courses add to the usability of these distance education programs. (Para.4) 围绕课程设立的论坛和网络社区增加了这些远程教育项目的可用性。本句中，过去分词短语 built around courses 做定语，修饰 forums and online communities。

7. It is a self-serving assertion coming from the online education provider, no doubt, but if we consider the fact that online learning is increasingly implemented as a training tool in corporations, the argument might already ring true. (Para.4) 毫无疑问，这是网络教育提供者为自身利益而给出的说法，但是如果我们知道网络学习被越来越多地用作公司的培训工具，这个说法听上去就可能令人信服了。
要搞清楚 assertion 和 argument 指的是同一观点，即本段开始句。

8. More productive key takeaways were the diversity of registrants, the apparent interest of non-traditional learners, and the innovation that results from this type of experimentation. (Para.7) 更富有成效的主要收益是注册者的多样性、非传统学习者们显而易见的学习兴趣和这种实验所带来的创新。

 **Exercises**

### I. Reading Comprehension

*Answer the following questions according to the article.*

1. What does this article talk about?
   _____

2. Who will take online courses?
   _____

3. Tell the benefits of online learning, one sentence for each:
   a. _____

b. _____
   c. _____
   d. _____
   e. _____
4. Web-based education is promising since _____,
   but at the same time it is lackluster because _____.
5. What are the reasons for people to choose online courses? List at least three reasons.
   a. _____
   b. _____
   c. _____
6. What can online education bring to the education system?
   _____
7. Will online learning replace the classroom according to this article? Why?
   _____

## II. Vocabulary Development

***A. Try to answer the questions after each of the following sentences with the context clues.***

1. Change is most evident in higher education, where massive open online courses (MOOCs) account for a growing share of academic content, but exactly how much *disruption* can we expect from online learning?
   → What does the word "disruption" mean here?

2. Allowing students to take courses on their own time, at their own pace, online learning systems are far more convenient than *their* in-person counterparts.
   → Who are the in-person counterparts?
   → What does the italic word "their" refer to?

3. But researchers Andrew Ho and Isaac Chuang say these low completion rates are not cause for concern; indeed *they* are a misleading metric.
   → What is a misleading metric?

4. For-profit colleges were early adopters of online learning, since *it* allowed *them* to attract customers who were otherwise unlikely to attend any sort of higher education.
   → What does it refer to?
   → What kind of customers are attracted?

→ What does the word "them" refer to?

5. More productive key *takeaways* were the diversity of registrants, the apparent interest of non-traditional learners, and the innovation that results from this type of experimentation.

→ What does the word "takeaways" mean?

**B. Fill in the blanks with proper words.**

1. Would you be comfortable _____ a family that smokes cigarettes?
2. We are _____ the cusp of a global revolution in teaching and learning.
3. I think the fact that so many of you are here tonight is a vote of confidence _____ our local performers.
4. I'm sure the audience has a host _____ questions for our team of experts.
5. I believe it is better to handle things _____ one's own pace than to plunge into it.

### III. From Reading to Speaking

MOOC is popular now. Universities are offering or plan to offer online courses to their students. But which one do you prefer, online teaching or classroom teaching? Form groups and debate.

**Topic:** Should online teaching take over classroom teaching?

# Reading Strategy

## 提问式阅读法（1）

不管用什么语言阅读报纸、杂志，其阅读的顺序应该是一致的，即先读大标题（headline）和副标题，确定本篇是讲什么的，确定自己是否对此感兴趣，以及感兴趣的程度，然后决定是否阅读，或快速浏览，或部分阅读，或全文仔细阅读。

大标题通常是一篇文章中心思想的高度浓缩。那么，根据标题进行提问，然后到文中去寻找答案，即"问题—解决法（problem-solving）"应该是一个快速抓住文章中心思想的有效方法。要注意的一点是：所提问题应该围绕主题内容，而不是某个词的词义。根据标题提问的问题通常由 why、what、when、who 和 where、how 等开头。

带着问题阅读实际上就是"有目的地阅读"。这是快速理解并掌握信息的必备能力。这种"提问式阅读法"有助于整体理解文章，而不是只懂"只言片语"，所谓"只见树木，不见森林"。

**例**　Evaluating Good Corporate Citizenship

Being a good company increasingly means more than just making a profit.

**解析**　看到这个标题后，可围绕标题关键词问如下问题：

* How can corporate citizenship be evaluated?

* Why does being a good company increasingly mean more than just making a profit?

* How important is good citizenship to a company?

* What should a company do to build up good corporate citizenship?

* What's the relationship between citizenship and profit?

带着这些问题去文中找答案，会发现这正是文章所要论述的主要观点。但是通常会有些问题在文章中找不到答案，便需要你再找有关文章阅读。

**练习**　请根据下列标题提问：

1. Your Call. Everybody's Business.
2. The Poverty of Affluence: Choosing Our Success.
—When Robert Reich noticed that work was costing him his personal life, he stepped down as US secretary of labor to reflect on what "success" really means.

Unit 1　Education

 **Reading 2**

# No Grades, No Timetable: Berlin School Turns Teaching Upside Down[1]

*By Philip Oltermann*

[1] Anton Oberländer is a persuasive speaker. Last year, when he and a group of friends were short of cash for a camping trip to Cornwall, he managed to talk Germany's national rail operator into handing them some free tickets. So impressed was the management with his chutzpah that they invited him back to give a motivational speech to 200 of their employees.

1. Who is Anton Oberländer?

[2] Anton, it should be pointed out, is 14 years old.

2. Then how did he achieve this ability?

[3] The Berlin teenager's self-confidence is largely the product of a unique educational institution that has turned the conventions of traditional teaching radically upside down. At Oberländer's school, there are no grades until students turn 15, no timetables and no lecture-style instructions. The pupils decide which subjects they want to study for each lesson and when they want to take an exam.

3. What did the institution do?

4. What is the upside-down education like?

[4] The school's syllabus reads like any helicopter parent's nightmare. Set subjects are limited to maths, German, English and social studies, supplemented by more abstract courses such as "responsibility" and "challenge". For challenge, students aged 12 to 14 are

5. What is a helicopter parent?

6. What do these abstract courses teach?

---

1. Adopted from *The Guardian*, Jul. 1, 2016

given €150 (£115) and sent on an adventure that they have to plan entirely by themselves. Some go kayaking; others work on a farm. Anton went trekking along England's south coast.

7. Why are these courses offered?

[5] The philosophy behind these innovations is simple: as the requirements of the labour market are changing, and smartphones and the Internet are transforming the ways in which young people process information, the school's headteacher, Margret Rasfeld, argues, the most important skill a school can pass down to its students is the ability to motivate themselves.

[6] "Look at three or four year olds—they are all full of self-confidence," Rasfeld says. "Often, children can't wait to start school. But frustratingly, most schools then somehow manage to untrain that confidence."

[7] The Evangelical School Berlin Centre (ESBC) is trying to do nothing less than "reinvent what a school is", she says. "The mission of a progressive school should be to prepare young people to cope with change, or better still, to make them look forward to change. In the 21st century, schools should see it as their job to develop strong personalities."

[8] Making students listen to a teacher for 45 minutes and punishing them for collaborating on an exercise, Rasfeld says, was not only out of sync with the requirements of the modern world of work, but counterproductive. "Nothing motivates students more than when they discover the meaning behind a subject of their own accord."

8. Then can students learn from these courses?

[9] Students at her school are encouraged to think up other ways to prove their acquired skills, such as coding a computer game instead of sitting a maths exam. Oberländer, who had never been away from home for three weeks until he embarked on his challenge in Cornwall, said he learned more English on his trip than he had in several years of learning the language at school.

9. So what do the schools in other states do?

[10] Germany's federalised education structure, in which each of the 16 states plans its own education system, has traditionally allowed "free learning" models to flourish. Yet unlike Sudbury, Montessori or Steiner schools, Rasfeld's institution tries to embed student self-determination within a relatively strict system of rules. Students who dawdle during lessons have to come into school on Saturday morning to catch up, a punishment known as "silentium". "The more freedom you have, the more structure you need," says Rasfeld.

10. What is the strict rule?

11. Why did the school do so?

[11] The main reason why the ESBC is gaining a reputation as Germany's most exciting school is that its experimental philosophy has managed to deliver impressive results. Year after year, Rasfeld's institution ends up with the best grades among Berlin's gesamtschulen, or comprehensive schools, which combine all three school forms of Germany's tertiary system. Last year's school leavers achieved an average grade of 2.0, the equivalent of a straight B— even though 40% of the year had been advised not to continue to abitur, the German equivalent of A-levels, before they joined the school. Having opened in 2007

12. What are the results?

13. What is *gesamtschulen*?
14. What are the all three school forms?

with just 16 students, the school now operates at full capacity, with 500 pupils and long waiting lists for new applicants.

[12] Given its word-of-mouth success, it is little wonder that there have been calls for Rasfeld's approach to go nationwide. Yet some educational experts question whether the school's methods can easily be exported: in Berlin, they say, the school can draw the most promising applicants from well-off and progressive families. Rasfeld rejects such criticisms, insisting that the school aims for a heterogenous mix of students from different backgrounds. Thirty per cent of students have a migrant background and 7% are from households where no German is spoken.

[13] Even though the ESBC is one of Germany's 5,000 private schools, fees are means tested and relatively low compared with those common in Britain, at between €720 and €6,636 a year. About 5% of students are exempt from fees.

[14] However, even Rasfeld admits that finding teachers able to adjust to the school's learning methods can be harder than getting students to do the same.

[15] Aged 65 and due to retire in July, Rasfeld still has ambitious plans. A four-person "education innovation lab" based at the school has been developing teaching materials for schools that want to follow the ESBC's lead. About 40 schools in Germany are in the process of adopting some or all of Rasfeld's methods. One in Berlin's Weissensee district recently let a student trek across the Alps for a challenge project. "Things are only getting started,"

15. Why is the school so popular now?

16. Why do the experts have this question?

17. What kind of students does ESBC receive?

18. What plans?

Unit 1　Education

says Rasfeld.

[16] "In education, you can only create change from the bottom—if the orders come from the top, schools will resist. Ministries are like giant oil tankers: it takes a long time to turn them around. What we need is lots of little speedboats to show you can do things differently."

19. What does giant oil tanker mean?

 **Useful Expressions**

| | |
|---|---|
| set subjects | 固定科目 |
| to be out of sync with | 与……不一致 |
| of one's own accord | 自愿地，主动地 |
| the tertiary system | 高等教育制度 |
| school leavers | 不继续上大学的高中毕业生 |
| word-of-mouth success | 口碑 |
| at full capacity | 满负荷，全力 |

 **Notes**

1. So impressed was the management with his chutzpah that they invited him back to give a motivational speech to 200 of their employees. (Para.1)（铁路）管理部门对他这种胆大妄为印象非常深刻，乃至后来又邀请他来给他们的 200 名员工做了一次励志演讲。本句为倒装句，正常语序为：The management was so impressed with...

2. **Helicopter parent** (Para.4) is a colloquial, early 21st-century term for a parent who pays extremely close attention to his or her child's or children's experiences and problems, particularly at educational institutions. They are so named because, like helicopters, they

19

hover closely overhead, rarely out of reach, whether their children need them or not.

3. In the 21st century, schools should see it as their job to develop strong personalities. (Para.7) 在21世纪，学校应该把培养学生坚强的个性当作自己的责任。
it 为形式宾语，替代 to develop strong personalities。

4. The Evangelical School Berlin Centre (ESBC) is trying to do nothing less than "reinvent what a school is"... (Para.7) ESBC 就是要重塑学校的形象……
nothing less than 指"等于，完全，正好是，恰恰是"。

5. The more freedom you have, the more structure you need... (Para.10) 你要的自由越多，你所需要的制度就越多……
structure 意为"制度，体系"。

6. Even though the ESBC is one of Germany's 5,000 private schools, fees are means tested and... (Para.13) 尽管 ESBC 是德国5 000多家私立学校之一，但它的收费是根据（对学生家庭）收入调查结果而定的……

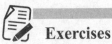 **Exercises**

**I. Reading Comprehension**

*Answer the following questions according to the article.*

1. What does this article mainly talk about?
   _____

2. Why is Anton Oberländer mentioned at the beginning of the article?
   _____

3. (T/F) Anton Oberländer is so self-confident and capable that he becomes the model of the school.

4. To _____, the Evangelical School Berlin Centre (ESBC) carries out an upside-down education system that allows students to _____.

5. (T/F) The students in ESBC are free to decide what subject they want to learn, at what time they want to take tests and whether they are going to work hard.

6. The traditional classroom teaching is ineffective because _____.

Unit 1  Education

7. ESBC receives students from _____ with _____ fees.
8. What is the biggest challenge for ESBC to carry out this upside down education system?
   _____
9. According to the president of ESBC, how can a school reform achieve success?
   _____
10. The Berlin's upside down education is to make students learn through _____.

## II. Vocabulary Development

**A. Try to answer the questions after each of the following sentences with the context clues.**

1. The *philosophy* behind these innovations is simple.
   → The synonym of the word "philosophy" is _____.

2. But frustratingly, most schools then somehow manage to *untrain* that confidence.
   → What do most traditional schools do with students' inborn confidence?

3. Even though 40% of the year had been advised not to continue to *abitur*, the German equivalent of A-levels, before they joined the school.
   → What can a student possibly do if he continues to *abitur*?
   → What does "40% of the year" refer to?

4. Ministries are like giant oil tankers: it takes a long time to turn *them* around
   → What does the word "them" refer to?
   → Paraphrase this sentence.

**B. Fill in the blanks with proper words.**

1. The new hospital is short of cash _____ medical equipment.
2. The president felt disappointed since he failed to talk the minister _____ supporting his educational reform.
3. China embarks _____ a massive programme of reform.
4. Most of the famous public schools are operating _____ full capacity while some less qualified ones are in need of students.
5. Under current US labor law, home-care workers are exempt _____ minimum wage and overtime pay requirements.

## III. From Reading to Speaking

If you had the chance to reform the school education, what were you going to do? Describe your idea about the school education to the class.

## Reading 3

# "Hire" Education: A Vocational Model Succeeds[1]

*By Audrey Schewe*

[1] Have you ever used what you learned in high school to get a job? Ask the graduates of Central Educational Center in Croweta County, Georgia, and you'll likely get a resounding "yes".

[2] Mark Whitlock runs the CEC, a publicly funded charter school that opened in August 2000. "Our mission is to ensure a viable 21st century workforce," Whitlock said.

[3] Like all public schools, CEC must meet state standards and its students are required to take all state standardized tests. However, as a charter school, CEC has the flexibility to tailor its curriculum to meet the changing needs of the business community.

[4] "CEC is about change in the workplace," says Whitlock. "In the 1960s and 1970s, most jobs could be accessed with a general high school diploma or less. Today, most jobs require something beyond high school—though not necessarily a four year degree—and generally technical in nature."

[5] Coweta County witnessed this change in the late 1990s, when the Yamaha Motor Manufacturing Corporation, a long-time employer, considered relocating its expanded operations.

[6] "Their message to our community was that we are not sure locally if we have the skilled workforce that we need," explains Whitlock.

[7] In response to message like this from various local employers, a study group comprised of country business, education and community leaders joined forces to address their individual yet interrelated needs.

[8] The group's findings were consistent with national data, notes Whitlock. "Workers have less supervision, so more independence is required; businesses have more automation, so more technical skills are required, and

---

1. Adopted from *CNN*, Mar. 7, 2007

we have a new global customer base, so workers need to relate to people across many different barriers."

[9] In addition, business leaders wanted a higher level of work ethic—a demand also not unique to Coweta County.

[10] A recent National Association of Manufactures study found that 69 percent of businesses cited "inadequate basic employability skills" such as attendance, timeliness and work ethic as the most common reason for rejecting job applicants.

## A new model for vocational education

[11] The study group's findings resulted in a new concept for high school education, realized in the opening of CEC in August 2000.

[12] "CEC is a joint venture among businesses, the Coweta County School System and West Central Technical College," explains Whitlock.

[13] With CEC designed and operated on a business model, Whitlock is known as the CEO rather than the principal. CEC teachers are referred to as directors, and students are called team members.

[14] Coweta high school students can spend part of their high school career at CEC, taking courses such as welding, graphic communications, electronics, computer networking and health occupations.

[15] But unlike traditional vocational education programs, CEC integrates higher academic standards with higher levels of technical and career proficiency.

[16] "The difference here," explains Whitlock, "is that we have high school age students taking classes with college curriculum, college instructors and college clinical rotations."

[17] Students who dual-enroll with West Central Technical College can earn college credit and even receive credit toward significant portions of an associate's degree prior to high school graduation.

[18] Another major difference between CEC and previous vocational programs is the emphasis on work-based learning.

[19] Partnerships with nearly 200 local businesses provide CEC students with real-world experiences such as unpaid internships, job shadowing and apprenticeships.

[20] VistaCare, one of the nation's leading hospice providers, is a CEC business partner. CEC students seeking certification as a Certified Nursing Assistant may shadow VistaCare's hospice

registered nurse.

[21] "The fact that we have the opportunity to get to know these potential employees before we hire them helps us to reduce employee turnover and helps to increase our patient satisfaction scores," said Vicki Kaiser, director of professional relations for VistaCare. "We are truly growing our own future workforce."

[22] Jeannie Davis, an area manager for ResourceMFG, a company that specializes in placing skilled and semi-skilled workers in the manufacturing industry, stresses the charter school's emphasis on work ethic as a reason for the success of its students.

[23] "Our customers complain that they have the huge attendance and performance issues," says Davis, "At CEC, students receive a work ethic grade (in addition to a course grade)—they are evaluated on attendance, ability to get along with others, how they work in a team and their willingness to participate."

[24] CEC meets the needs of the local economy while also meeting the needs of its students.

[25] As a high school junior, Mary King Tatum job-shadowed in hospitals and nursing homes as part of her health occupations courses at CEC. Senior year, she dual-enrolled in West Central Technical College. Prior to graduating from high school, she received her nursing assistant certification.

[26] "A lot of my peers were smart kids who assumed that if you were going to CEC it was because you weren't that smart, or that you didn't want to go to a four-year college," says Tatum. "But by my senior year, they could see how the CEC classes were really relevant."

[27] For hornors students Toby Hughes, CEC provided an opportunity to get the practical training that he needed to enter the computer networking industry. Hughes was hired by a computer networking company in his senior year. "After I graduated from high school," says Hughes, "they put me on salary for $52,000 and promoted me to Operations Manager—I was only 18 years old!"

## Useful Expressions

| | |
|---|---|
| a publicly funded charter school | 公立学校 |
| state standardized tests | 州标准化考试 |
| the business community | 商业社会 |
| relocate its expended operations | 重组其扩大的业务 |
| vocational education program | 职业教育 |
| work ethic | 职业道德 |
| job shadowing | 实习 |
| clinical rotations | 临床实习 |
| employee turnover | 雇员更替率 |
| put sb. on salary for... | 给某人……工资 |

## Notes

1. ... that we are not sure locally if we have the skilled workforce that we need, ... (Para.6) ……我们不能确定当地是否有我们需要的技术工人/劳动力……

2. In response to message like this from various local employers, a study group comprised of country business, education and community leaders joined forces to address their individual yet interrelated needs. (Para.7) 为了应对从当地各老板那里得来的信息，一个由国家企业、教育和社区领导组成的小组联合起来处理他们各自但又相互关联的需求。过去分词短语 comprised... leaders 做定语，修饰 group。

3. The study group's findings resulted in a new concept for high school education, realized in the opening of CEC in August 2000. (Para.11) 这个研究小组的调查结果形成了一种高中教育的新理念，而 2000 年 8 月 CEC 的开设则使得这种理念得以实现。过去分词短语 realized... 做定语，相当于 which was realized...

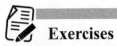 **Exercises**

### I. Reading Comprehension

*Complete the following sentences according to your understanding of the article.*

1. CEC is an educational center which _____.
2. CEC is opened in response to _____.
3. Unlike traditional school, CEC is a joint venture among 1)_____,
   2)_____, and 3)_____, with the principal as 4)_____,
   teachers as 5)_____, and students as 6)_____.
4. The modern business community needs workers of 1)_____,
   2)_____, 3)_____ and 4)_____.
5. CEC benefits both _____ and _____.
6. CEC is different from traditional vocational educational programs in that it
   a. _____,
   b. _____.
7. The high school students attending CEC can earn _____ when graduating from high school.
8. One of the most important reasons for the success of CEC is that it emphasizes _____.

### II. Vocabulary Development

*A. Decide the meaning of the italics according to the contexts.*

1. ..., as a charter school, CEC has the flexibility to *tailor* its curriculum to meet the changing needs of the business community.
   A. make clothes    B. become    C. adjust           D. train
2. ..., a study group comprised of country business, education and community leaders joined forces to *address* their individual yet interrelated needs.
   A. speak to    B. name    C. emphasize        D. deal with
3. VistaCare is a CEC business partner. CEC students seeking certification as a Certified Nursing Assistant may *shadow* VistaCare's hospice registered nurse.
   A. cover    B. follow    C. work as an intern    D. influence
4. "Our customers complain that they have the huge attendance and performance *issues*,"...
   A. problems    B. topics    C. supplying        D. results

**B. Fill in the blanks with proper words.**

1. None of these social problems is unique _____ this country.
2. Such behavior may result _____ the manager being asked to leave.
3. The speaker is referred to _____ an up-coming politician.
4. It is a good thing to integrate the tradition _____ modern arts.
5. They've got everything ready prior _____ the opening ceremony.

## III. From Reading to Speaking

Albert Einstein said, "Education is what left after you have forgotten everything you learned at school." Form groups to debate. Firstly, two groups will discuss what exact argument you are going to debate over the following topic.

**Topic:** What should elementary education teach?

# Part C
# Unit Assignments

1. People have been discussing about education all the time. These three articles reflect some very important issues about education. Write an essay to discuss (1) problems in education in general, or (2) some specific problems in education. Don't forget to give your suggestions to solve the problem. And try to use the information and the language from this unit as much as possible.
2. List the questions you have after reading these three articles.
3. List at least 10 expressions and sentence structures with meanings you have found in this unit, and try to make your own sentences with them.

# Unit 2

# Science and Technology

# Part A
# Lead-in

# Go Humans: Lee Sedol Scores First Victory Against Supercomputer[1]

Go grandmaster wins fourth showdown of five-match series against Google's artificial intelligence, AlphaGo.

*By Mark Tran*

[1] The rise of the machines came to a halt, temporarily at least, when the champion Go player Lee Sedol beat a computer program on Sunday to prevent a whitewash after losing the first three games.

[2] AlphaGo, developed by the Google subsidiary DeepMind, has an insurmountable lead in the series, but Sedol's win restored some human dignity. Fans of the ancient Chinese board game cheered when AlphaGo quit after five hours and Lee was greeted by applause from journalists at the post-match news conference at a Seoul hotel.

[3] "This one win is so valuable and I will not trade this for anything in the world," said Lee, one of the best Go players in the world.

---

1. Adopted from *The Guardian*, Mar. 13, 2016

[4] The 33-year-old South Korean Go grandmaster said he believed he had found two weaknesses in the artificial intelligence (AI) program. AlphaGo seemed to have a problem with unexpected moves, indicating the machine lacked the ability to deal with surprises, and appeared to have more problems playing with a black stone, Lee said.

[5] In Go, a game for two, players take turns putting black or white stones on a 19-by-19 grid. The winner is the player who surrounds more territory than his or her opponent. Despite its seeming simplicity, the permutations of Go vastly exceed those in chess.

[6] The first move of a game of chess offers 28 possibilities; the first move of a game of Go can involve placing the stone in one of 361 positions. A game of chess lasts around 80 turns while Go games can last 150.

[7] Lee played with a white stone on Sunday. For the final match of the series, scheduled for Tuesday, Lee has offered to play with black, saying it would make a victory more meaningful.

[8] The DeepMind founder Demis Hassabis said the loss was a valuable learning tool and would help identify weaknesses in the program that needed to be fixed.

[9] "It's a real testament to Mr Lee's incredible fighting spirit and he was able to play so brilliantly today after three defeats," said Hassabis, a 39-year-old Briton who started the AI research firm and who plays master-level chess.

[10] Before the five-game series, Lee exuded confidence. "I don't think it will be a very close match," he said. "I believe it will be 5–0, or maybe 4–1. So the critical point for me will be to not lose one match."

[11] Experts did not expect an AI program to beat a human professional for at least a decade, until AlphaGo beat a European champion player last year. Lee, however, was considered a much more formidable opponent.

[12] Google executives say Go offers too many possible moves for a machine to win simply through brute-force calculations, unlike chess, in which IBM's Deep Blue famously beat former world champion Garry Kasparov in 1997. Instead, they said, AlphaGo was designed to approximate human intuition by studying old matches and using simulated games to hone itself independently.

[13] In the past, Hassabis described Go as "a bit of a holy grail for AI research", though he stressed on Saturday that Lee's defeat should not be seen as a loss for humanity. "Our hope is that in the long run we will be able to use these techniques for many other problems," Hassabis said.

**Answer the following questions.**

1. What game did Lee Sedol win?

2. Who is Lee Sedol?

3. What is AlphaGo?

4. How can the supercomputer compete with human?

5. Is there any other artificial intelligence that has defeated human?

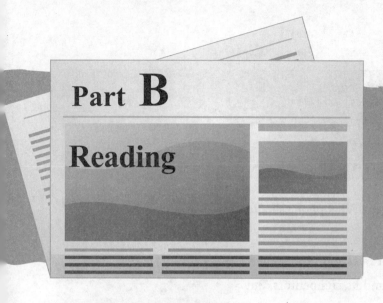

# Navigate the Jungle of Tech Ecosystems[1]

How Apple, Google and Microsoft are racing to control your digital life—from phone to home-automation system.

By David Pogue

## Pre-reading Questions

1. What is an ecosystem?
2. What should be a tech ecosystem like?
3. What is a digital world?
4. How does the digital technology influence your life?

*Your questions before reading the article:*
1. _____
2. _____
3. _____
4. _____
5. _____

---

1. Adopted from *Scientific American*, Dec. 1, 2015

> *Words you know related to this topic:*
> *smart phone* _____ _____ _____
> _____ _____ _____ _____

[1] The question is no longer, "What phone should I get?"

1. Why is this no longer a question?

[2] That *was* an important question immediately after the arrival of the iPhone and its competitors. But now it's time to admit that today's smartphones (and tablets) are nearly identical. Apple and Google (maker of Android phone software) have copied each other's ideas so completely that the resultant phones are incredibly close in looks, price, speed and features.

2. What is the question then?

3. Then any difference?

[3] These days the Apples, Googles and Microsofts of the world are competing on a different battlefield: They're racing to build the best, most enticing ecosystem. Each is creating a huge archipelago of interconnected products and services. It's about velvet handcuffs: Making it easy for you to embrace its offerings and as hard as possible to switch to a rival's.

4. What is the ecosystem for?

[4] A typical ecosystem includes hardware (phone, tablet, laptop, smartwatch, TV box); online stores (music, movies, TV, e-books); synchronization of your data across gadgets (calendar, bookmarks, notes, photographs); cloud storage (a free online "hard drive" for files); and payment systems (wave your watch or phone instead of swiping a credit card).

5. What does the ecosystem include?

[5] For consumers, the choice is now what suite of products they like best.

*Unit 2* **Science and Technology**

[6] If you're one of these companies, though, you've got a difficult decision to make: Should you open up your services to people who use your competitors' products? Say, let an iPhone user load an Outlook calendar or let a Microsoft Band smartwatch wearer sync data to an Android tablet.

[7] On one hand, making your software available to those outside your ecosystem could introduce the rest of the world to the superiority of your products—and possibly bring in new consumers.

[8] On the other hand, you would lose the exclusivity of those services as a lure. Why would anyone switch if she or he can already get the best of a rival's offerings?

[9] So what approach are the giants taking? It's a mixed bag.

[10] Apple is the most closed. In general, it writes apps only for iPhones and iPads. You can't make a FaceTime call to an Android or Windows Phone, for example, or run the Apple Maps app on those devices (not that you'd want to). And you can't use the Apple Watch with anything but an iPhone. You *can*, however, use Apple's iCLoud (online file storing and sync services) on a Windows device—but not on one using Google's Android.

[11] Google goes to great lengths to make its wares available to other platforms. If you have an iPhone, you can use Google's apps (Gmail, Chrome, Google Maps), services (Docs, Sheets, Slides) and even digital store (Books, Music, Newsstand). The services and store are also available to Mac, Windows and Linux users. You

6. What will happen if I open up it?

7. What is in the bag?

can even link an Android Wear smartwatch with an iPhone.

[12] Then there's Microsoft. Microsoft Office is available for just about anything with a screen, as are many of its mobile apps.

[13] Why such inconsistency?

[14] It helps to understand the individual corporate motives. Although these three companies offer so many similar (okay, almost identical) gadgets and services, each is actually running on an entirely different business model. Apple is primarily in the business of selling hardware; Microsoft, software; Google, ads. Each has different considerations in calculating what to open up.

[15] And Apple and Google continue to branch out; both now offer, if you can believe it, software for your car dashboard and home-automation system designed to work with their respective smartphones. Surely Microsoft won't be far behind. Samsung boasts its own cluster of competitive products and linked services. Even Amazon—once a *bookstore*, for goodness's sake—now makes phones, tablets and TV boxes.

[16] You, the consumer, should be delighted by this direction. Perhaps dismayed by all the duplication of effort but happy there's competition, which always begets innovation (and often lower prices). And you should be pleased that overall the trend seems to be for these companies to make more of their services accessible, no matter which phone or computer you own.

8. Why don't they develop the apps that can run on all the services?

9. What are their motives?

10. What direction?
11. Why happy?

[17] Eventually the ecosystems may well become nearly identical, too. Maybe at that point, the question will once again become, "What phone should I get?"

 **Useful Expressions**

| | |
|---|---|
| digital ecosystems | 数字生态系统 |
| cloud storage | 云存储 |
| payment systems | 支付系统 |
| swipe a card | 刷卡 |
| bring in | 带来，引进 |
| get the best of | 从……获得最大好处 |
| go to great lengths to do sth. | 竭尽全力做某事 |

 **Notes**

1. It's about velvet handcuffs: Making it easy for you to embrace its offerings and as hard as possible to switch to a rival's. (Para.3) 这就好比天鹅绒制的手铐：让你很容易就接受它提供的产品，但要想换用其对手的产品就没那么容易了。
冒号表示解释、说明什么是 velvet handcuffs。冒号后面是一个并列结构：make it easy to embrace 和 as hard as possible to switch。

2. Say, let an iPhone user load an Outlook calendar or let a Microsoft Band smartwatch wearer sync data to an Android tablet. (Para.6) 例如，让苹果使用者下载 Outlook 的日历，或者让戴 Microsoft 智能手表的人与安卓平板同步数据。
本句中，两个 let 的宾语后接不带 to 的不定式，做宾补。

3. On one hand, making your software available to those outside your ecosystem could introduce the rest of the world to the superiority of your products—and possibly bring in new

consumers. (Para.7) 一方面，使你的生态系统之外的人能够使用你的软件，让这世界上其他人了解你的产品的优势——而且同时也可能带来新用户。

本句的主语为现在分词短语 making your software available to those outside your ecosystem。谓语是两个并列谓语 introduce 和 bring in。

4. Microsoft Office is available for just about anything with a screen, as are many of its mobile apps. (Para.12) 只要带屏幕的东西都能使用 Microsoft Office 以及它的其他移动应用。

as 连接词，表示"同样地"，可以替代前面的 available for just about anything with a screen。

5. Perhaps dismayed by all the duplication of effort but happy there's competition, which always begets innovation (and often lower prices). (Para.16) 也许会对所有这些重复劳动表示惊愕，但也很开心因为有了竞争，有了竞争就会有创新（而且经常还会有低廉的价格）。

本句为无主语句，根据上下文得知主语是 you, the consumer 被省略了。而 effort 则指代那几个公司的研发与产品；which 引导一个非限制性定语从句，说明前面的 competition。

6. And you should be pleased that overall the trend seems to be for these companies to make more of their services accessible, no matter which phone or computer you own. (Para.16) 你会高兴地看到，大趋势是不管你使用哪款手机或电脑，这些公司都会让它们所提供的服务更易获得。

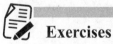

## Exercises

### I. Reading Comprehension

*Answer the following questions according to the article.*

1. What are digital ecosystems?

2. How do the big tech companies lure the customers?

3. Why is it called the jungle of tech ecosystem?
   _____

4. What can the customers do with the ecosystems provided by those tech companies?
   _____

5. While their phones are almost similar in 1)_____, 2)_____, 3)_____ and 4)_____, different companies focus on different businesses:
   a. Apple    _____
   b. Google   _____
   c. Microsoft _____
   d. Samsung  _____
   e. Amazon   _____

6. While the customers need to know_____,
   the companies need to decide _____.

7. How will the customers feel about the duplication of efforts of these tech companies? Why?
   _____

## II. Vocabulary Development

*A. Try to answer the questions after each of the following sentences with the context clues being italicized.*

1. Each is creating a huge *archipelago* of interconnected products and services.
   → What is each company creating?

2. It's about velvet handcuffs: *making it easy for you to embrace its offerings and as hard as possible to switch to a rival's.*
   → Why is it called a velvet handcuff?

3. You, the consumer, should be delighted by *this* direction.
   → What are the customers happy about?

4. Apple is the most *closed*.
   → How is Apple's system?

5. Microsoft Office is available for just about anything with a screen, *as* are many of its mobile apps.
   → What Microsoft products and services can we get for our smartphones?

**B. Fill in the blanks with proper words.**

1. Service stations use petrol as a bait to *lure* motorists _____ the restaurants and other facilities.
2. Twins are mostly close _____ looks but different in tempers.
3. I don't like Apple products because it is a trouble to sync the photos and music in my computer _____ my phone.
4. The school authority is now taking efforts to bring _____ new deans for some of the departments.
5. The next step of our job is to run our app _____ different mobile devices.

## III. From Reading to Speaking

**TV talk show:** Two or three people form a group. Turn this article into a talk show. Suppose one of you is the TV presenter/host. The other or other two are the guests from Apple and Samsung or Microsoft, etc. mentioned in this article. The topic of the show is about "the digital ecosystem". The task of the host is to ask questions and comment a little bit. The guests are to answer questions. Try to include all the information of the article with questions and answers. When performing, try your best to speak, making it a real show.

# Reading Strategy

## 提问式阅读法（2）

任何篇章都是为了传达某种信息，而篇章中的每一句话甚至一个词都是为传达某种信息服务的，句子和句子之间都有相互关联的逻辑关系。是否能够理解并掌握所传达的信息就要看读者是否能够积极地进行阅读。那么，在阅读文章正文时可以使用"提问式阅读法"，即读者在阅读时不停地就所读句子进行提问，然后在上下文（即前后句）中寻找答案。（参见每单元文章右边的 margin questions，试着自己提些问题。）也就是说，读者在阅读过程中主动与作者展开对话，主动索取信息。一般说来，每个篇章甚至每句话，都包含有如下五个方面的信息：Who、What、Why (How)、When、Where。每读一句话，读者都可以就其中的不定因素（内容）或整句话进行提问（Who、What、Why、How、When、Where），然后在后面的句子中寻找答案。如此读完后所获得的信息是有逻辑的相互连接的整体，而不是支离破碎的细枝末节。

**例** Ever since there have been Commerce secretaries (nearly a century), they've made such phone calls (*What call?*→): strands in a global web of American dealmaking. But what makes this one (*Which one?*) noteworthy—and worthy of suspicion to Bush's enemies—is the date on which it took place, Oct. 15 (*What happened on Oct. 15?* →), for Lay knew that his world was about to fall apart. (*Why?* →) In a conference call with Wall Street analysts the next day, he would have to disclose that Enron had lost an astounding $618 million in the third quarter. More important, it would soon become clear that Enron had lost $1.2 billion in a labyrinth of partnerships that probably should have been—but weren't—counted on the company's books. (*The result of this fact?* →) Enron, one of the most innovative and admired companies in the world, was near collapse. (*How could this happen?*) Didn't Lay and Evans, an old friend in the Texas energy business, discuss the impending crisis? (*Did they?* →) They both say no. (*Really?*) But investigators—at least on Capitol Hill—will want to ask, preferably in a hearing on TV. (*What will the investigators want to ask?*)

**解析** 以上段落中的黑斜体是根据前一句关键词所提的问题，箭头指向答案。其中第 2 个问题是提问指代词 (this) 的，根据其使用功能，它是前指，指代的上一段中提到的一次电话。第 6 个和第 9 个问题（尤其是第 9 个）也没有答案，可期望在下一段中找到。通过问题，我们便可以了解到本段落句子之间的关联，以及和上一段落、下一段落的关联。尤其是段落结尾的问题和下一段落联系紧密。

**练习** 模仿上例，就下面的文字内容提问，并找到答案。

The fund could behave in two ways. It could decide that it is primarily a humanitarian effort, treating victims' families as in need of relief rather than of compensation. The average awards per life might then be fairly small, but would reflect the plight of the family (so a fireman's widow with four children would do better than a rich banker's childless one). But it is more likely that the fund will see itself as a jury dispensing compensation in a wrongful-death case. A formula that incorporates lost future income would yield larger awards (and also favour the banker's wife).

# The Robots Are Coming[1]

*By Kevin Maney*

[1] Snow White was prescient. In a scene from the 1937 Disney movie, she gets a team of birds and cute woodland animals to clean the dwarfs' house while she warbles "Whistle While You Work".

1. Why does the author talk about Snow White here at the beginning?

[2] A decade or two from now, that's going to be how you take care of your house—except the work will be done by small robots, each built for a single purpose. They will hover in the air to pick up clutter, climb walls to wash windows and scuttle under furniture to vacuum while you sit back with a cappuccino and binge-watch Breaking Bad reruns.

2. Who are they?

[3] Outdoors you'll find a robot swarm cleaning the streets, trimming trees, and watering plants. Little packages will get dropped off by flying quad-rotor drones, probably emblazoned with the familiar Amazon.com smiley face. For the big stuff—like, say, a refrigerator—an autonomous vehicle guided by Google technology will pull into your driveway, and a hulking Google bot with six legs will carry the fridge up your stairs and gently set it where you want it.

[4] Over Thanksgiving, Amazon unveiled its drone delivery project on *60 Minutes*, and in no time the jokes and indignation were flying:

3. Then how does the public respond to this new technology?

---

1. Adopted from *Newsweek*, Dec. 11, 2013

Hunters will grab their shotguns and use the drones like clay pigeons.

The drones will short out and fall from the sky by the hundreds when a rainstorm blows in.

Walmart is working on drones that kill Amazon drones.

[5] Then, days after Amazon's reveal, Google went public with its new robotics unit, run by Andy Rubin, the whiz who created Google's Android operating system. The message: Google's investment is no lark. Robots are for real.

[6] In fact, Google and a lot of other companies believe robots today are like cell phones back when they were the size of bricks and cost $6,000. It may take 10 or 20 years, but before long everybody is going to have a robot—or several.

[7] These robots will not look the way most people expect—they won't walk and talk like C3PO or Rosie from *The Jetsons*. An all-purpose humanoid robot doesn't make much sense. As tech thinker Kevin Kelly wrote, "To demand that [intelligent robots] be human-like is the same flawed logic as demanding that artificial flying be birdlike, with flapping wings."

[8] Instead, the world will gradually acquire many kinds of robots, each designed and built to most effectively carry out a particular task in a way that saves humans time, money or drudgery.

[9] The Amazon drones would do that. Loaded with artificial intelligence, they promise to deliver small items faster than any human could.

4. What are the jokes about?
5. What are people angry about?

6. Who is Andy Rubin?
7. Whose message is it?

8. What do robots look like according to most people?

9. What will be the coming robots look like?
10. What kind of robots will we have?

[10] Google's experimental driverless cars are robots. One day, a delivery truck driver will seem as redundant as an elevator operator.

[11] Robotics and artificial intelligence are tough fields, but there's so much research lab and start-up money going into it, we'll get the technology right long before we sort out how to integrate robots socially, legally and practically. It's less difficult to imagine delivery drones working than to imagine the New York sky darkened by thousands of the things carrying everything from shoes to Chinese take-out.

[12] "We'll solve those kinds of problems when the benefits to society become large enough," says Colin Angle, chief executive officer of iRobot, maker of the granddaddy of consumer robots, the Roomba vacuum cleaner. Angle notes that when cars were invented, they were insanely dangerous and disruptive and widely hated.

11. What kind of problems will come with the benefits of robots?

[13] Society is already a long way into robotics and we often don't know it. I recently visited some family members who own an enormous farm in Saskatchewan. They handle the harvest with just three people and a giant combine that has so many smarts, the driver mostly rides along and never touches anything. In another decade, the smarts will be so good that the farmer can stay inside and play the commodities market while machines do all the work in the field.

12. What shows that robots have already been in our life?

13. How will the robots be probably developed in the near future?

[14] Robot news will keep coming. A company called Knightscope just unveiled its robotic security guard. It could roam a warehouse floor at night, its

camera keeping an eye out for anything unusual, its chemical sensors sniffing for leaks.

[15] A startup called Play-i is making toy-like bots that can teach a 5-year-old how to program bots. And you know where that will lead in two decades: 25-year-olds who can invent ever more intelligent bots.

[16] Rodney Brooks, who runs the robotics lab at the Massachusetts Institute of Technology and co-founded iRobot with Angle, has a new robotics company, Rethink Robotics. It is making an inexpensive industrial robot that is simple to train and can work alongside a human. An entrepreneur, for instance, could set one up in her garage and teach it to make something, creating a small automated factory.

14. How can a robot work with a human?

[17] Brooks and Angle have long believed the Roomba was the first phase of the "robot-enabled home". They followed Roomba up with the Scooba floor-washing robot, and promise more along those lines—perhaps a window-washing bot, or a clothes-folding bot. (iRobot won't give specifics.) The bots will likely all be wirelessly connected to each other, and to a kind of "head butler" robot that takes commands from its owner and hands out tasks to the many mini-bots.

15. What is a "robot-enabled" home?

[18] It's no fantasy, Angle insists. This is the not-too-distant future.

[19] Plus, it's a whole lot easier than getting birds and squirrels to do your dusting.

Unit 2  Science and Technology

## Useful Expressions

| | |
|---|---|
| by the hundreds | 数以百计 |
| an all-purpose humanoid robot | 全能类人机器人 |
| make sense | 有意义 |
| toy-like bots | 玩具机器人（bots = Robots） |
| start-up money | 启动资金 |
| the not-too-distant future | 不远的将来 |
| a whole lot | 相当多 |

## Notes

1. They will hover in the air to pick up clutter, climb walls to wash windows and scuttle under furniture to vacuum while you sit back with a cappuccino and binge-watch Breaking Bad reruns. (Para.2) 当你坐在那儿喝着卡布奇诺，追看《绝命毒师》时，他们会在空中盘旋着捡废品，爬上墙擦窗户，或者钻到家具下面去吸尘。

   binge: indulge in an activity, especially eating, to excess 放纵、沉溺（于做某事），常用以形容无节制行为，binge watching 追剧（无节制地狂看某部电视连续剧）。binge drinking 酗酒；binge eating 大吃大喝

2. For the big stuff—like, say, a refrigerator—an autonomous vehicle guided by Google technology will pull into your driveway, and a hulking Google bot with six legs will carry the fridge up your stairs and gently set it where you want it. (Para.3) 对于冰箱之类的大个儿的东西，装有谷歌导航的自主车会驶入你家的车道，然后一个六腿谷歌机器人帮你把冰箱搬上楼，轻轻地放到你指定的位置。

3. *60 Minutes* (Para.4): An American newsmagazine television program broadcast on the CBS television network. Debuting in 1968, the program was created by Don Hewitt, who chose to set it apart from other news

47

programs by using a unique style of reporter-centered investigation.

4. C3PO (Para.7): 简称 3PO，是《星球大战》系列中的角色，作为一个神经质的、多愁善感的礼仪机器人，C-3PO 是由沙漠行星塔图因上一个九岁的天才用废弃的残片和回收物拼凑而成的。年轻的安纳金·天行者打算让这个自制机器人帮助他的妈妈西米。在材料有限的情况下，安纳金做的这个机器人确实算很出色了。不过他没有外壳，他的零件和线路都露着，所以 C-3PO 只得生活在"赤裸"的羞耻之中。

5. Rosie (Para.7): the electronic maid and housekeeper on the TV show The Jetson's (a prime-time animated sitcom that originally aired from 1962–1963 and again from 1985–1987, and *Jetsons: The Movie*, a 1990 American animated musical comic science fiction comedy-drama film). High TechScience.org owns several "Rosie the Robots" including the 2010 Hallmark Special Edition version which speaks several lines from her stint on *The Jetson's*.

6. Kevin Kelly (Para.7): The Digital visionary, the publisher of the Whole Earth Review, executive editor at WIRED, founder of visionary nonprofits, and writer on biology and business and "cool tools". He's admired for his new perspectives on technology and its relevance to history, biology and religion. He made a series of TED talks on technology:
(1) *How Technology Evolves*
(2) *The Next 5,000 Days of the Web*
(3) *Technology's Epic Story*

7. It's less difficult to imagine delivery drones working than to imagine the New York sky darkened by thousands of the things carrying everything from shoes to Chinese take-out. (Para.11) 比起被成千上万的搬运货物的东西搞得黑压压的纽约上空，这些货物从鞋子到中餐外卖，无所不及，想象一下工作着的无人送货机还是不太难的。
本句为比较状语从句，两个谓语相比较。从句中的过去分词短语做定语，修饰 the New York sky。现在分词短语做定语，修饰 the things。

8. It could roam a warehouse floor at night, its camera keeping an eye out for anything unusual, its chemical sensors sniffing for leaks. (Para.14) 夜里它会在仓库里到处转悠，它的照相机会时刻留意任何异常，它的化学传感器会嗅

到泄露。
本句含两个分词独立结构用以解释伴随性状态：its camera keeping..., its chemical sensors sniffing...。

9. An entrepreneur, for instance, could set *one* up in her garage and teach it to make something, creating a small automated factory. (Para.16) 比如，一个企业家能够在她的车库里安一个，然后教它制作，这样就创造了小型的自动化工厂。
本句后半部分的分词做状语，表示主句部分所带来的结果。

10. The bots will likely all be wirelessly connected to each other, and to a kind of "head butler" robot that takes commands from its owner and hands out tasks to the many mini-bots. (Para.17) 机器人们有可能通过无线传输来相互连接，并和一个类似"总管"机器人相连接。这个总管机器人从它的主人那里领命令，然后把任务传达给其他许多微型机器人。
本句中，that 引导的定语从句修饰 "head butler" robot。

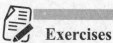

## Exercises

### I. Reading Comprehension

*Finish the following tasks according to your understanding of the article.*

1. What kind of robots are coming?
   _____

2. When will the robots come?
   _____

3. In the 1937 Disney movie, Snow White had animal robots to clean the dwarfs' house. ( T/F )

4. Now Walmart is working on drones that kill Amazon drones. ( T/F )

5. In future, the robots can be various kinds and not human-like. ( T/F )

6. Which company unveiled its robotic security guard?
   A. Google            B. Knightscope
   C. Amazon            D. not mentioned in the article

7. Which is NOT a future robot according this article?
   A. driverless cars          B. flying quad-rotor drones
   C. C3PO                     D. window-washing bot
8. The world will gradually acquire many kinds of robots which can effectively _____
   _____.
9. If there are Google's experimental driverless cars, a delivery truck driver will seem _____.
10. We can sort out how to integrate robots socially, legally and practically when _____
    _____.

## II. Vocabulary Development

**A. Try to answer the questions after each of the following sentences with the context clues being italicized.**

1. Then, days after Amazon's reveal, Google went public with its new robotics unit, run by Andy Rubin, the whiz *who* created Google's Android operating system.
   → Who is Andy Rubin?

2. Society is already a long way into robotics and we often don't know *it*.
   → How is the development of robots?

3. An entrepreneur, for instance, could set *one* up in her garage and teach it to make something, creating a small automated factory.
   → How can an entrepreneur make his factory automated?

4. They handle the harvest with just three people and a giant combine that has so many *smarts*, the driver mostly rides along and never touches anything.
   → Who will handle the harvest mainly?

**B. Fill in the blanks with proper words.**

1. Is there any chance you could drop _____ this package for me at the post-office?
2. Now it is a fashion for some people, say celebrities, not to go public _____ their marriage.
3. Loaded _____ their military equipment, they are ready for fighting.
4. The dog kept an eye _____ for the strangers and barked.
5. The salesmen usually follow up a letter _____ a visit.

## III. From Reading to Speaking

Design a robot. Then you can introduce your robot to the class, including its look, features and etc. Or you can act it out with a partner to show what your robot can do.

# Reading 3

## The Simple, Free Solution to Asia's Myopia Epidemic[1]

By Madison Park

[1] It's not just Asia. Around the world, we're becoming collectively more near-sighted. Near-sightedness, or myopia, means nearby objects appear clearly, but those farther away look blurry.

[2] The rates of myopia have doubled, even tripled, in most of East Asia over the last 40 years, researchers say. Several places like Hong Kong and Singapore City have rates in the 80%. In South Korea, myopia rates among 20-year-olds have leaped from 18% in 1955 to over 96% myopia in 2011.

[3] And it's a global issue—rates of myopia are also rising in Western nations like Germany and the United States.

[4] "It's about 40% in the US, compared to about 25% in the 1970s," said Dr. Michael Chiang, clinical spokesperson for the American Academy of Ophthalmology.

[5] But researchers say reducing risk of myopia is easy, free and readily-available: Get some sunlight.

[6] Sometimes, though, the easiest solutions are the hardest to implement.

## It's not the obvious scapegoat.

[7] The epidemic of myopia amongst East Asians has triggered cultural questions about why so many young people develop vision problems.

[8] Many have long believed that reading, studying or staring at your phone caused short-sightedness. And there's the usual grumblings that young people spend way too much time glued to their screens.

[9] But researchers are focusing on a different cause.

[10] "If children get outside enough, it doesn't matter how much they study they do. They don't become myopic," said Ian Morgan, researcher at Australian National University.

---

1. Adopted from *CNN*, Apr. 6, 2015

[11] Researchers say kids and teens need to get sunlight during the critical years of their development while their eyeballs are still growing.

[12] The mechanics of how sunlight protects their eyes are not clearly understood. One theory suggests that sunlight triggers the release of dopamine in the retina; another speculates that blue light from the sun protects from the condition.

[13] The solution is simple. Have kids "spend more time outside, have less demands (from) the schools and relax a bit", said Seang Mei Saw, professor of epidemiology at the National University of Singapore.

## Negotiating outdoors time

[14] But studying and play time are often at odds with each other.

[15] In Asian cultures where there is heavy emphasis on education and hyper-competitiveness, forcing playtime is easier said than done.

[16] "The problem is teachers and parents are probably not going to let kids," said Dr. Nathan Congdon, professor at the Zhongshan Ophthalmic Center at the Sun Yat Sen University in China. "There's a limit to how many hours kids can go outside."

[17] There have been some attempts to protect children's eyesight.

[18] In China, students have been mandated by its education ministry to perform daily eye exercises. Since 1963, rows of students sit at their desks and massage the pressure points around their eyes as a revolutionary-era anthem blares through the PA system.

[19] Despite these eye exercises, rates of myopia in urban China have soared to nearly 90%, according to recent studies.

[20] "China has among the highest rates of myopia and it's the only country in the world that does eye exercises, so it's probably not working all that well," said Congdon.

[21] Their effectiveness has been doubted by experts in China, but the exercises remain a part of the students' daily experience.

## Is it really a big deal?

[22] Myopia may seem like a minor inconvenience. People have to deal with glasses, contact lenses and even laser eye surgery. But researchers say there are serious implications of such high rates of myopia among young people.

[23] In Singapore, 82% of 20-year-olds are myopic. By the time these young adults hit their 60s, many of their vision

problems are likely to get worse.

[24] "They grow older and the epidemic is then in older adults," said Saw, head of the myopia unit at the Singapore Eye Research Institute.

[25] As people age, they can become at higher risk for severe eye disorders such as high myopia, glaucoma (optic nerve damage), cataracts (clouding of the lens) and retinal detachment. These conditions could lead to vision loss and blindness.

## Students in see-through schools

[26] To negotiate the expectations of parents and classes, researchers are experimenting ways to help students get increased exposure to sunlight.

[27] One of the studies underway is the "bright light classroom" where the school's walls and ceilings are made of see-through plastic that allows in light. Hundreds of students attend this unusual elementary school in Guangdong province.

[28] "It's a potential way to increase the amount of light, in hopes of preventing myopia and allow kids to continue (their) education without inconvenience for them," Morgan said.

[29] Researchers want to measure the rates of myopia among students in these "bright light classrooms" compared with those in traditional classes.

[30] Building schools costs money—especially experimental see-through schools. But researchers say there are low-cost solutions.

[31] In a study, teachers locked the students out of the classroom during recess and lunch time. In that 2013 study, students boosted their time in sunlight by 80 minutes during the school day. Fewer children in that school became nearsighted compared with those from another school that didn't follow such a policy.

[32] Researchers hope with greater understanding of this condition, far-sighted policies could save the next generation of children's eyesight.

**Useful Expressions**

| | |
|---|---|
| vision problems | 视力问题 |
| way too much | 太……，太多 |
| at odds with | 与……不一致 |
| easier said than done | 说起来容易做起来难 |
| eye exercises | 眼保健操 |
| recess time | 课间休息 |
| far-sighted policies | 有远见的政策 |
| the PA system | 体育课 |

**Notes**

1. And there's the usual grumblings that young people spend way too much time glued to their screens. (Para.8) 大家经常抱怨的是年轻人盯着屏幕的时间太长了。本句意思为：People are grumbling that young people have spending way too much time glued to their screens.

2. In Asian cultures where there is heavy emphasis on education and hyper-competitiveness, forcing playtime is easier said than done. (Para.15) 在特别强调教育与高竞争力的亚洲文化中，强迫玩耍时间是说起来容易做起来难。本句中，where 引导的定语从句修饰 cultures。easier said than done 说起来容易做起来难。

3. The problem is teachers and parents are probably not going to let kids. (Para.16) 问题是老师和家长可能不会让孩子们（出去玩）。本句为表语从句，is 后面省略了 that。同时 let kids 后面省略了宾语补足语，补全应是 let kids play/go out。

*Unit 2*  Science and Technology

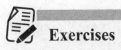 **Exercises**

### I. Reading Comprehension

*Answer the following questions.*

1. What is the Asia's myopia epidemic?

2. Why is it called "an epidemic"?

3. What is the simple and free solution to Asia's myopia epidemic?

4. What is the rationale of this simple and free solution?

5. What are the possible causes and consequences of the myopia epidemic according to the researchers?

6. Why does it become an epidemic when the solution is simple and free?

7. What are the eye exercises performed in China?

8. What is a see-through school?

### II. Vocabulary Development

**A. What do the italic words in the following sentences refer to?**

1. Near-sightedness, or myopia, means nearby objects appear clearly, but *those* farther away look blurry.
2. And *it*'s a global issue.
3. Is *it* really a big deal?
4. Researchers say kids and teens need to get sunlight during the critical years of *their* development while *their* eyeballs are still growing.
5. In that 2013 study, students boosted *their* time in sunlight by 80 minutes during the school day.

**B. Fill in the blanks with proper words.**

1. Allen, don't glue _____ the tube all day long.

2. Most workers focus _____ working for pay and benefits that reward them in the short term, but is often disastrous in the long.
3. I think I'm _____ odds with you over the supplying plan.
4. Whether or not you're at risk _____ a heart attack, you should probably try to quit smoking.
5. _____ hopes of doing a better job next time, I've interviewed four professionals who have focused on the subject.

**III. From Reading to Writing**

**Survey:** Suppose you are asked to write a report about the existing eyesight situation of the students in your school. First, you should do a survey to collect data about the students' eyesight. Write at least 6 questions for your survey. The following questions are for your reference:

What is your eyesight?

If near-sighted, when did you get near-sighted?

What are the cause of your near-sightedness?

How do you fix your vision?

If not near-sighted, how can you get a good vision?

Do you have any suggestions to those near-sighted?

Second, randomly ask 15 students and 5 teachers these questions and take down their answers.

Third, sort out the data and analyze them.

Last, write your report. Do remember to provide solutions or your suggestions at the end.

# Part C
# Unit Assignments

1. Science and technology might be a major part of modern life, which actually have produced some problems. Write an essay to discuss the effects of science and technology on human. Support your opinion with evidence. And try to use the information and the language from this unit.
2. List the questions you have after reading these three articles.
3. List at least 10 expressions and sentence structures with meanings you have found in this unit, and try to make your own sentences with them.

# Unit 3

# Disasters

# Part A Lead-in

## Yangtze Basin Hit by Flooding with Storms Spanning 1,000 Miles[1]

At least 33 million people in China affected by floods and 180 reported killed.

By Nicholas Lee (MetDesk)

[1] Severe flooding hit the Yangtze river basin in China this week. Heavy rainfall ranging from 100 to 500mm in some areas fell across seven provinces, the storms stretching 1,000 miles. More than 180 people were reported killed by the flooding, dozens were missing and, overall, 33 million people were affected. Twenty three people were killed by a single mudslide in Guizhou province.

[2] India and Pakistan also suffered damaging floods over the weekend, and more than 60 people died. The floods hit during Ramadan prayers; a busy mosque was washed away and 70 houses were destroyed or severely damaged in the Pakistan province of Chitral. There were fears of further monsoon rains to come.

[3] Meanwhile, the Australian city of Adelaide had its wettest day in 75 years on

---

1. Adopted from *The Guardian*, Jul. 12, 2016

Monday, with more than 50mm recorded in 24 hours in some suburbs. The emergency services dealt with hundreds of callouts for flooding issues, while wind gusts in excess of 60mph knocked out power supplies to 2,000 homes, thanks to fallen trees. Nearby Mount Lofty even had a rare, brief, dusting of snow.

[4] Finally, holidaymakers in Spain may have found the summer weather a little too intense in recent days, as extreme heat sent the mercury soaring. Heat warnings were issued for much of the country, with many areas exceeding 40C. Hottest of all was Cordoba, in the province of Andalusia, where a high of 44.5C was measured on Sunday—about 8C above normal. In Madrid afternoon temperatures have topped 33C every day since 20 June.

 **Answer the following questions.**

1. What happened in the Yangtze river basin in China this week?
   _____

2. What did India and Pakistan suffer this weekend?
   _____

3. How wet was Adelaide, Australia this week?
   _____

4. What kind of weather did the holidaymakers experience in Spain?
   _____

5. What killed 23 people in Guizhou, China?
   _____

# Different Natural Disasters, Same Risky Human Habits[1]

*Editorial*

**Pre-reading Questions**

1. What are natural disasters?
2. Can you list any natural disasters in the recent decade?
3. What should we do when natural disasters come?
4. What can we do to help the people who have experienced the natural disasters?

*Your questions before reading the article:*

1. _____
2. _____
3. _____
4. _____
5. _____

---

1. Adopted from *USA TODAY*, Oct. 26, 2007

## Unit 3   Disasters

> *Words you know related to this topic:*
> **earthquake** _____ _____ _____
> _____ _____ _____ _____
> _____ _____ _____

[1] By most measures, Hurricane Katrina and the California wildfires have little in common except gale-force winds and human misery.

1. What are the differences?

[2] Katrina was a disaster of greater magnitude. Estimates of Katrina-related fatalities start at 1,800, compared with about a dozen in the wildfires. And, along with Hurricane Rita, Katrina destroyed 350,000 homes, compared with about 1,600 in California.

[3] What's more, the reaction of emergency officials, at all levels of government, has been more competent this time. On the political front, President Bush, who famously flew over Louisiana in its first hours of need without landing, touched down Thursday in Southern California.

[4] But one thing that the wildfires share with Katrina is that both natural disasters were made worse by the propensity of people to build homes in high-risk areas. Katrina's economic impact was magnified by development along the vulnerable Gulf Coast. Similarly, the wildfires have been particularly brutal in newly developed communities in fire-prone scrublands and dry pine forests.

2. What propensity?
3. Where are these high-risk areas?

[5] A USA TODAY analysis Thursday found that 55,000 people have moved into new communities hit by the fires—just since 2000. Building in fire-prone

4. How many people have come to live in these areas?

areas has been running at twice the state average. And one devastated community in Orange County has tripled its population in the past seven years to 22,329.

[6] Something is obviously wrong here. Public safety is one of the most important functions of state and local governments, which can and should do more to discourage people from moving to dangerous areas, and minimizing the consequences when they do.

[7] To some degree, market forces can help address the problem. Higher homeowners' insurance rates discourage building in unsafe areas. But this approach only goes so far.

[8] In the Gulf, it's impossible to even talk of market forces because they have been distorted by the federal flood insurance program, which encourages people to build in flood and hurricane-prone areas by offering them insurance and rates well below what is necessary to cover the costs of catastrophes.

[9] In California, with its ample incomes and sky-high housing costs, expensive homeowners' insurance is just part of the cost of living that people tolerate. In fact, development in high-risk areas has been driven in large part by unaffordable housing in more established neighborhoods.

[10] Partial solutions for Southern California include stricter building codes and more aggressive land use planning. Homes and businesses could be built, or retrofitted, with fire-retardant materials and protective features to prevent embers from getting inside. Owners could also be required to prune away brush.

5. Then why do people like living in these dangerous areas?
6. What is wrong?
7. Then why is building still allowed in these areas?
8. What should the government do?
9. What kind of market forces?
10. How far?
11. Why?
12. What is the program about?
13. How can this program encourage people to live in dangerous areas?
14. Then is there any other solution?
15. What are the details of the solution?

[11] These precautions would likely run into considerable resistance. As a general rule, homeowners don't like to be told what to do with their homes, particularly when that involves spending money. And buying land to set aside as buffers is not cheap.

[12] But these fires show that each homeowner, and each community, is affected by others. Fire-prone neighborhoods are not only more likely to catch fire, they also can serve as the kindling for spreading infernos.

[13] Without aggressive action to control development and reduce the threat in the most vulnerable areas, future fires might still not rival Katrina's destructiveness, but they certainly will bring human suffering on an ever-escalating scale.

16. Are these solutions effective?

## Useful Expressions

| | |
|---|---|
| gale-force winds | 大风 |
| emergency officials | 紧急救援官员 |
| high-risk areas | 高危地带 |
| newly developed communities | 新开发区 |
| fire-prone areas | 易发生火灾地区 |
| a devastated community | 灾区 |
| homeowners' insurance rates | 房主保险率 |
| run into resistance | 遭到反对 |

**Notes**

1. Estimates of Katrina-related fatalities start at 1,800, compared with about a dozen in the wildfires. (Para.2) 与森林大火中十几个死亡人数相比，卡特里娜的死亡人数至少为1,800。
compared... = compared with the fatalities of about a dozen in the wildfires

2. But one thing that the wildfires share with Katrina is that both natural disasters were made worse by the propensity of people to build homes in high-risk areas. (Para.4) 但是森林大火与卡特里娜有一点是相同的，即这两种自然灾害都是因为人们喜欢在高危险区盖房子而变得更加严重。
本句为表语从句，其中不定式 to build homes in high-risk areas 做定语，说明解释 the propensity。

3. Public safety is one of the most important functions of state and local governments, which can and should do more to discourage people from moving to dangerous areas, and to minimize the consequences when they do. (Para.6) 公共安全是州政府及地方政府的重要功能之一，它应该尽力阻止人们搬往危险地区（居住），从而把他们搬去这些地区导致的后果降到最小。
which 引导一个非限制性定语从句，进一步解释 governments 的作用，其中谓语动词 do 后面有两个不定式 to discourage 和 to minimize，表示 do more 的目的。

4. In fact, development in high-risk areas has been driven in large part by unaffordable housing in more established neighborhoods. (Para.9) 事实上，这些高危地区的开发绝大部分是因为大家买不起那些老区（如闹市区）的房子。

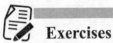 **Exercises**

**I. Reading Comprehension**

*Complete the following sentences according to the text.*

1. Hurricane Katrina and California wildfires are _____.
2. The author uses Hurricane Katrina and California wildfires to _____.

3. Hurricane Katrina and California wildfires are similar in a) _____, and b) _____.
4. One of the governments public tasks is public safety which _____ _____, while the federal flood insurance program is to _____.
5. There are some solutions like 1) _____ and 2) _____, but it 3) _____.
6. According to the author, everyone in the fire-prone area is _____.
7. This article tells us that humans now tend to _____, which can _____ different natural disasters.

## II. Vocabulary Development

### A. Answer the questions after each of the following sentences.

1. Building in fire-prone areas has been running at twice the state average.
   → How have the buildings in fire-prone areas developed?

2. Public safety is one of the most important functions of state and local governments, which can and should do more to discourage people from moving to dangerous areas, and minimizing the consequences when they do.
   → The last word "do" means _____.

3. To some degree, market forces can help address the problem.
   → The word "address" means _____.

4. These precautions would likely run into considerable resistance.
   → What would be resisted?

### B. Fill in the blanks with proper words.

1. She discourage her husband _____ borrowing money.
2. No one was injured when a tornado touched _____ near this area.
3. You'd better prune _____ all those dry grapevines as soon as possible.
4. Try to set _____ some time to do some mending.
5. He served _____ an adviser to the company after retirement.

## III. From Reading to Speaking

Work in groups and discuss: (1) What kind of human habits can probably endanger nature and environment? (2) How can these habits endanger nature? After discussion, form a report and present to the class.

# Reading Strategy

## 长句的理解

"提问式阅读法"同样适用于对长句的理解。复杂长句是阅读过程中的一大障碍。实际上，复杂长句就等于一个小语篇（mini-passage），它的各个相互关联的附属部分共同传达一个主要的信息。读者在遇到这类句子时，首先找出句子的主干（主、谓、宾），然后就主干部分的不定因素提问，答案是在本句的其他附属成分里寻找，在寻找答案时遇到不定因素同样提问，并进一步寻找答案，如此一步一步地提问，就很容易理解句子的整体意义，并记住重要的细节。

**例** He is interested in a wide range of customs that is found in various cultures, and his object is to understand the way [in which these cultures change and differentiate], the different forms [through which they express themselves], and the manner [in which the customs of peoples function in the lives of the individuals].

**解析** 第一个逗号后面的 and 连接的是两个并列句。先看第一句：主干是 He is interested in a wide range of customs，其中 a wide range 是不定因素，有两个问题可以问：What range? Why is it wide? 答案即是 that 引导的定语从句。第二句相对复杂一些：两个逗号及 and 连接的是三个并列部分，主干应该是：his object is to understand the way..., the different forms..., and the

manner...。这里三个宾语都是特指，用 the 限定，但都不含具体内容，所以就应该有问题，即：What kind of way? What kind of form? What kind of manner? 答案分别在其后面方括号中的定语从句中。理解这个句子的关键在于要对 and 这个词的功能非常熟悉，且敏感，再就是在阅读过程中对一些看上去并非生词的概念名词的具体内容要"打破砂锅问到底"。

**练习** 请就下面句子的一些词提问并在句中找到答案：

The mental conversation could take the form {of asking and answering the questions [formed from the headings] or reading the summary, [which lists the main ideas in the chapter], and trying to fill in the details for each main idea}.

1. What is the form?

2. What are the questions about?

3. What is the summary?

# Reading 2

# Midwest Floods Leave Red Cross in the Red[1]

Agency turns to loans as disaster relief fund is completely depleted.

[1] The American Red Cross, its disaster funds already depleted by scandals and dwindling donations thanks to the souring economy, has run out of money as it struggles to meet the needs of tens of thousands of Midwestern flood victims, agency officials said.

[2] The agency said its domestic Disaster Relief Fund had been wiped out by flood relief expenses that had reached $15 million by Monday. With a balance of zero in the fund, the Red Cross will now seek loans to support its 2,500 staff workers and volunteers on the ground in Wisconsin, Iowa, Illinois and Missouri, the officials said.

[3] "That's putting this in the category of a very significant disaster for the Red Cross, historically, when you would look at what we spend on relief efforts," Joe Becker, the agency's senior vice president of disaster services, said in a conference call with reporters Monday.

[4] "We have had a large number of midsize disasters or 'silent' disasters that have cost us a considerable amount of money where we've not been able to raise what it's cost us to provide that service,"

1. How much does the Midwestern flood need?

2. What should the Red Cross do?

3. What is the significant disaster for the Red Cross?
4. What efforts do they do?

---

1. Adopted from *MSNBC News*, Jun. 17, 2008

Becker said.

[5] Hundreds of homes have been destroyed and tens of thousands of people have been evacuated by floods that local officials describe as the worst in several generations after the Cedar, Iowa and Mississippi rivers breached their banks.

[6] "It's unreal. It's unreal. We were only hoping to get the 100-year [flood], and they hammered us with more than a 500-year," said Jeff Gillick, a Cedar Rapids, Iowa, city employee.

[7] The floods have been blamed for at least 22 deaths, 17 of them in Iowa, where state officials told NBC News that they expected damage in excess of $1 billion. President Bush was briefed on the damage and was scheduled to visit the area for a firsthand look later this week.

[8] Bush said he would seek emergency legislation in Congress to allocate disaster relief funds for the Midwest. But that process will take time, leaving the Red Cross as the primary resource for now.

## Soaring costs meet diminishing donations

[9] Jeff Towers, the Red Cross' chief development officer, said that the cost of the Midwestern relief effort could soar as high as $40 million. That bill follows closely on the heels of two busy months for the agency, which conducted 27 disaster operations in April and May.

[10] But the Red Cross has managed to raise only $3.2 million, Towers said, because donors squeezed by the economy are finding it difficult to contribute more

5. Then what's the government's response?

6. Which bill?
7. How busy was it?

money.

[11] The agency has also found it hard to win back the confidence of individual and corporate donors after a series of scandals, including criticism of its handling of donations after the terrorist attacks of Sept. 11, 2001, and its response to Hurricane Katrina.

8. Why is it hard to win back the confidence?

[12] The Red Cross laid off a third of its national headquarters staff—about 1,000 people—in February to address a budget deficit of nearly $200 million, and it fired its president in November for having an extramarital affair with a local director in Mississippi. The new president, Gail McGovern, is the agency's sixth in six years.

[13] Towers stressed that "the Red Cross remains committed to providing the scale of services that people expect of the Red Cross when disaster strikes". But with the disaster fund tapped out, "the way that we are doing that right now is taking out loans to fund our response," he said. "That's not a position we want to be in. It's obviously not sustainable."

 **Useful Expressions**

| | |
|---|---|
| disaster relief fund | 赈灾基金 |
| relief efforts | 赈灾工作 |
| emergency legislation | 紧急立法 |
| chief development officer | 首席开发官，开发总监 |
| a budget deficit | 预算赤字 |

Unit 3   Disasters

**Notes**

1. The American Red Cross, its disaster funds already depleted by scandals and dwindling donations thanks to the souring economy, has run out of money as it struggles to meet the needs of... (Para.1) 美国红十字会的灾难基金由于受到丑闻及因经济恶化而逐渐减小的捐款的影响而被耗尽，当面对中西部地区成千上万个需要救助的洪水难民时，却已经没有钱了……
   本句为 as 引导的时间状语从句，其中两个逗号之间为分词独立结构，作原因状语说明"钱没有了"的原因。thanks to 由于

2. "We have had a large number of midsize disasters or 'silent' disasters that have cost us a considerable amount of money where we've not been able to raise what it's cost us to provide that service,"... (Para.4) 我们遭遇了很多花去我们很多钱的中等的或者说不出口的灾难，但却没有能力筹集到这么多钱来应付这些灾难。
   where = whereas（但是），what... 引导 raise 的宾语从句，其中 that service = to deal with the midsize disaster or silent disaster that cost us a considerable amount of money。

3. ... because donors squeezed by the economy are finding it difficult to contribute more money. (Para.10) ……因为在银根紧的时候，捐献者们发现很难拿出更多的钱来了。
   squeezed by the economy = who are squeezed by the economy

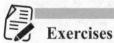
**Exercises**

**I. Reading Comprehension**

*Answer the following questions according to the text.*

1. What does this article mainly talk about?
   A. The Midwest floods                B. The finance of the Red Cross
   C. The scandals of the Red Cross     D. The relief efforts by the Red Cross
2. (T/F) The American Red Cross is running out of funds only because the disasters cost too much.

73

3. The fund of the Red Cross is used to support all the following EXCEPT _____.
   A. staff workers          B. volunteers
   C. emergency officials    D. disaster victims
4. (T/F) The Red Cross is still in short of money even after the government allocated disaster relief fund.
5. The red Cross has experienced a series of the following problems EXCEPT _____.
   A. public criticism of their handling the donation after Sept. 11, 2001
   B. public criticism of its response to Hurricane Katrina
   C. its former president's extramarital affair
   D. too many disasters to deal with
6. The present solution to the depleted fund of the Red Cross is to _____.

## II. Vocabulary Development

*A. Answer the questions after each of the following sentences with the context clues.*

1. "That's putting this in the category of a very significant disaster for the Red Cross, historically, when you would look at what we spend on relief efforts,"...
   → What is a very significant disaster for the Red Cross?
   → Why is it a disaster?

2. "We were only hoping to get the 100-year [flood], and they hammered us with more than a 500-year,"...
   → What does the word "they" refer to?

3. But that process will take time, leaving the Red Cross as the primary resource for now.
   → What will take time?
   → Can the government allocate the relief fund immediately?
   → Who will do the relief work now?

4. "... the way that we are doing that right now is taking out loans to fund our response," he said. "That's not a position we want to be in. It's obviously not sustainable."
   → Tell what each "that" means here.

*B. Fill in the blanks with proper words.*

1. Cars are largely blamed _____ the disappointing environment.
2. Never spend _____ excess of your income.
3. The secretary was briefed _____ the secret cash payments.
4. Epidemics often follow _____ the heels of floods.

*Unit 3* **Disasters**

5. The unpleasant memory has been wiped _____ by the reunion of the family.

### III. From Reading to Speaking

There are quite a few charity groups or NGOs (Non-government Groups) or Funds home and abroad. They are offering help to those in need. But there are also many reports about the scandals involved in some of these groups. Try to find information about either scandals or charities of some of these groups, and then report to the class.

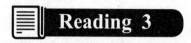

# Humans Add to Natural Disaster Risk[1]

Statistics reveal social trends that leave us more vulnerable.

By Ker Than

[1] Earth might seem like a more active and dangerous place than ever, given the constant media reports of multiple natural disasters recently. But a broader view reveals that it's not Mother Nature who's changed, but we humans.

[2] Drawn by undeveloped land and fertile soil, people are flocking to disaster-prone regions.

[3] This creates a situation in which ordinary events like earthquakes and hurricanes become increasingly elevated to the level of natural disasters that reap heavy losses in human life and property.

[4] Meanwhile, in any given year, the death toll at the hands of Mother Nature varies greatly, as do the sorts of major deadly events.

## How we die

[5] Of the estimated 61,000 people who have died this year due to natural disasters, more than 50,000 (according to today's estimate) were victims of the 7.6 earthquake that struck Pakistan Oct. 7. In 2004, by contrast, more than 60 percent of the total natural disaster deaths were caused by the tsunami in the Indian Ocean.

[6] So far, the distribution of natural disasters for 2005 is similar to that of 2004, said Debarati Guha-Sapir, director of the Center for Research on Epidemiology of Disasters, or CRED, headquartered in Brussels, Belgium. However, Guha-Sapir cautioned that it is still premature to make direct comparisons between the two years, noting that the Dec. 26 tsunami that struck Indonesia and killed 130,000 people came so late in the year.

[7] Other natural disasters for 2005 that have resulted in a major loss of life include:

---

1. Adopted from *Live Science*, Oct. 17, 2005

[8] An 8.7 magnitude earthquake that struck Indonesia on March 28, killing more than 1,600 people.

[9] Hurricane Katrina, which struck the Gulf Coast in late August, killing more than 1,200 people.

[10] Hurricane Stan, which triggered mudslides in countries throughout South America that killed a reported 1,153 people when it made landfall Oct. 4.

[11] Hurricane Katrina, which caused an estimated $200 billion dollars in damage, is the costliest natural disaster so far this year. It is also the costliest natural disaster in US history.

[12] All of these numbers pale greatly in comparison to deaths caused every year by war, famine and communicable diseases.

## Disasters increasing

[13] Along with the Office of US Foreign Disaster Assistance, CRED maintains an emergency disaster database called EM-DAT. An event is categorized as a natural disaster if it kills 10 or more people or leaves at least 100 people injured, homeless, displaced or evacuated. An event is also included in the database if a country declares it a natural disaster or if the event requires the country to make a call for international assistance.

[14] According to the EM-DAT, the tally of natural disasters reported each year has been steadily increasing in recent decades, from 78 in 1970 to 348 in 2004.

[15] Guha-Sapir said that a portion of that increase is artificial, due in part to better media reports and advances in communications. Another reason is that beginning in the 1980s, agencies like CRED and the US Agency for International Development began actively looking for natural disasters.

[16] "Like in medicine, if you go out into a village and look for cases you find much more than if you just sit back and let people come to you when they're sick," Guha-Sapir said.

[17] However, about two-thirds of the increase is real and the result of rises in so-called hydro-meteorological disasters, Guha-Sapir said. These disasters include droughts, tsunamis, hurricanes, typhoons and floods, and they have been increasing over the past 25 years. In 1980, there were only about 100 such disasters reported per year, but that number has risen to more than 300 a year since 2000.

[18] In contrast, natural geologic disasters, such as volcanic eruptions, earthquakes, landslides and avalanches, have remained steady in recent decades.

## What's going on?

[19] Scientists believe the increase in hydro-meteorological disasters is due to a combination of natural and human-caused factors. Global warming is increasing the temperatures of Earth's oceans and atmosphere, leading to more intense storms of all types, including hurricanes.

[20] Natural decadal variations in the frequency and intensity of hurricanes are also believed to be a contributing factor, as are large-scale temperature fluctuations in the tropical waters of the Eastern Pacific Ocean, known as El Nino and La Nina.

[21] People are also tempting nature with rapid and unplanned urbanization in flood-prone regions, increasing the likelihood that their towns and villages will be affected by flash floods and coastal floods.

[22] "Large land areas are [being] covered with cement, so this means the flow of water becomes very strong," Guha-Sapir said. "The runoff from the water can't get absorbed by the soil anymore, so it keeps collecting and rushing down, getting heavier and faster, and then you have much bigger floods."

[23] People aren't just putting themselves at risk for floods, but for natural disasters of all types, including earthquakes and storms like hurricanes and typhoons.

## Making disasters

[24] "As you put more and more people in harms way, you make a disaster out of something that before was just a natural event," said Klaus Jacob, a senior research scientists at Columbia University's Lamont-Doherty Earth Observatory.

[25] According to the World Bank's "Natural Disaster Hotspots: A Global Risk Analysis", a report released in March, more than 160 countries and regions have more than a quarter of their populations in areas of high mortality risks from one or more natural disasters.

[26] The good news is that the number of deaths from natural disasters has decreased substantially in recent decades, thanks to better disaster preparedness and prevention programs. But this statistic is tempered by the fact that more people are being injured, displaced or left homeless.

[27] "If you don't die, you need care," Guha-Sapir said. "To a certain extent, we prevent people from dying, but more and more people are affected."

Unit 3　Disasters

## Useful Expressions

| | |
|---|---|
| death toll | 死亡人数 |
| reap heavy losses | 导致重大损失 |
| communicable diseases | 传染病 |
| the Office of US Foreign Disaster Assistance | 美国国际开发署国外救灾办公室 |
| an emergency disaster database | 紧急灾难数据库 |
| hydro-meteorological disasters | 水文气象灾难 |
| natural geological disasters | 自然地质灾难 |
| a contributing factor | 成因 |
| flash floods and costal floods | 暴洪和海岸区洪水 |
| high mortality risks | 高死亡风险 |

## Notes

1. This creates a situation in which ordinary events like earthquakes and hurricanes become increasingly elevated to the level of natural disasters that reap heavy losses in human life... (Para.3) 这就造成了一种局势。在这一局势中，诸如地震、飓风等普通事件越来越上升到给人们生活和财产带来重大损失的自然灾难的水平。
This 指代上一句中 people are flocking to... 这一事实；that 引导定语从句，修饰说明 natural disasters。

2. ... it is still premature to make direct comparisons between the two years, noting that the Dec. 26 tsunami that struck Indonesia and killed 130,000 people came so late in the year. (Para.6) ……直接比较这两年还为时过早，因为12月26日袭击印尼，同时使130 000人丧生的海啸是在那年年底发生的。
分词短语 noting... 做状语，说明"为时过早"的原因。

3. People are also tempting nature

with rapid and unplanned urbanization in flood-prone regions, increasing the likelihood that their towns and villages will be affected by flash floods... (Para.21) 因为人类迅速而无计划的城市化使自然承担风险,从而也使他们的城镇更容易遭受洪水和……的侵害。
分词短语 increasing... 做状语,表示主句所陈述事实的结果,其中 that 引导定语从句,修饰说明 likelihood。

4. "As you put more and more people in harms way, you make a disaster out of something that before was just a natural event,"... (Para.24) "当你把越来越多的人置于危险境地时,你就把原先的自然现象变成了灾难。"……

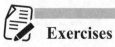

## Exercises

### I. Reading Comprehension

*Answer the following questions according to the text.*

1. How can humans add to natural disasters?
   _____

2. Why do these social trends leave us more vulnerable?
   _____

3. What can be categorized as natural disasters?
   _____

4. What natural disasters caused most death in 2005 and 2006?
   _____

5. The increase in natural disasters in recent years is partly 1)_____, which includes 2)_____ and 3)_____. And two-thirds of the increased disasters are 4)_____ called 5)_____, including 6)_____, 7)_____, 8)_____, 9)_____ and 10)_____.

6. What causes the increase in hydro-meteorological disaster?
   _____

7. To what extent can prevention programs help the human?

_____

## II. Vocabulary Development

### A. Answer the questions after each of the following sentences with the context clues.

1. ... in any given year, the death toll at the hands of Mother Nature varies greatly, as do the sorts of major deadly events.
   → Are there many different major disasters in a year recently?

2. All of these numbers pale greatly in comparison to deaths caused every year by war, famine and communicable diseases.
   → The word "communicable" means _____.
   → The word "pale" means _____.

3. ... a portion of that increase is artificial, due in part to better media reports and advances in communications.
   → The word "artificial" means _____.

4. The runoff from the water can't get absorbed by the soil anymore, so it keeps collecting and rushing down, getting heavier and faster, and then you have much bigger floods.
   → What does "it" refer to?

### B. Fill in the blanks with proper words.

1. During the National Day, people were flocking _____ the Olympic Park.
2. The banking crisis in America has resulted _____ the financial crisis in the whole world.
3. The government made this law _____ the concern over house pricing.
4. Individual students are singled _____ for praise at the end of the semester.
5. They temped him _____ a chance to travel in a strange land.

## III. From Reading to Writing

We humans are often supposed to be superior to the nature with a slogan that "human can conquer the nature". What is your view? Write an essay with no less than 150 words to explain your points.

# Part C
# Unit Assignments

1. Write a report to review the natural disasters in recent ten years in the world, and try to analyze the possible reasons or causes for these disasters. Give your suggestions to prevent the disasters.
2. List the questions you have after reading these three articles.
3. List at least 10 expressions and sentence structures with meanings you have found in these three articles, and try to make your own sentences with them.

# Unit 4

# Sports

# Part A
# Lead-in

## News Reading

## Li Jianrou Wins 500m Gold[1]

[1] SOCHI, Russia—In the slippery world of short track, China kept its grip solidly on the Olympic gold medal.

[2] Li Jianrou extended her country's dominance in the women's 500 meters Thursday, winning its fourth consecutive title after she was the only skater who didn't fall in the wild final.

[3] Three-time defending champion Wang Meng of China missed the Olympics after breaking her ankle last month. Li had little experience in the wild and woolly sprint, where getting off to a quick start is important. But she kept her cool while everyone else was falling around her.

[4] Li Jianrou won gold simply by staying on her feet in a crash-filled final.

[5] "I feel very lucky," Li said through a translator. She and one of her coaches cried tears of joy after China joined South Korea as the only countries to win the same short track event four Olympics in a row. The Koreans won the 3,000 relay in 1994, 1998, 2002 and 2006.

---

1. Adopted from *Associated Press*, Feb. 13, 2014

[6] "I cried because I was so excited," Li said. "My coach told me this medal is for Wang Meng as well, so I felt very moved."

[7] Li's victory made up for the surprising fall of teammate Fan Kexin in the semifinals.

[8] Arianna Fontana of Italy took the silver and Park Seung-hi of South Korea earned the bronze.

[9] Elise Christie of Britain caused the crash in the second turn of the opening lap when she veered into Fontana and sent both skaters spinning into the pads.

[10] "I saw Elise come in and thought I'd stop her, but she kept going," Fontana said. "This is short track, so that's what happens. When I was falling I was so sad, then I saw the Korean girl fell and I thought I could still get something so I got up as quickly as I could. I got my silver medal, but for me it's gold."

[11] Park got clipped and lost her balance going into the next turn. She fell into the sideboard, but got up and resumed skating. Li was closely trailing in last place when the chaos erupted. She took over the lead and went on to victory.

[12] "I had more speed so I tried to stay out of reach of the fourth-place skater (Li)," Christie said. "I tried to pass and got bumped by the girl on the outside (Fontana)."

[13] Park came across the line in last place, but Christie got disqualified, allowing Park to claim the bronze.

[14] In the semis, Fan didn't even complete the first lap of the sprint, catching her left blade as she skated near the front. She crashed on all fours into the crew of workers who maintain the ice between races. They scrambled onto the top of the pads to avoid being injured by Fan's long, sharp blades.

[15] Christie was lucky to be in the 500 final, surviving a photo finish to advance to the medal round after Fan's crash.

[16] Park was trying to give South Korea a victory in the only short track event it has never won.

[17] "It is such a great disappointment," Park said through a translator. "But it is also part of my destiny. I have to accept it."

[18] It was a tough day at the rink for the South Koreans. The men's team had a call going against them in the 5,000 relay semifinals after a crash involving Lee Ho-suk and American Eddy Alvarez.

[19] "The boys were not lucky," Park said. "I was not lucky either."

[20] The referees advanced the US team of Alvarez, J.R. Celski, Chris Creveling and Jordan Malone into the A final while the South Koreans were relegated to the B final.

[21] Lee was leading on the outside late in the race with his left hand down on the ice when it clipped Alvarez's right skate. That sent Alvarez and Lee sliding into the pads.

[22] "He slipped on his right and sat real deeply on his left, sticking his left arm out," Alvarez said. "It just so happened as I was crossing through, we collided. My hand and his skate. It didn't allow me to come through."

[23] "I was going for the pass. I was coming with more speed. I'm glad the refs caught that."

[24] There's a history of bad blood between the South Koreans and the US dating to the 2002 Salt Lake City Games. They believed Apolo Anton Ohno stole the gold from Kim Dong-sung, who finished first in the 1,500 meters but was disqualified for blocking. The animosity toward Ohno grew so heated that the entire American short-track team withdrew from a World Cup event held in South Korea in 2003, citing death threats against Ohno.

[25] But Sin Da-woon wasn't blaming the Americans after this latest tangle.

[26] "We moved into them," he said. "It wasn't the Americans' fault. There was a mix-up in the signs. If we were clear with the signals then we could have avoided this. It's a pity we couldn't advance."

[27] The US waited anxiously while the referees sorted out the chaos.

[28] "The moments between the fall and the call, there's a lot of doubt," Celski said. "Just disbelief that we didn't make it to the final. But our coach looked fairly confident."

[29] Viktor Ahn led his adopted country of Russia into the relay final, which will feature five teams because of the US getting in. The Netherlands, Kazakhstan and China

also made the final.

[30] In a surprise, Canada fell in its 5,000 semi and didn't make the final. The team of Michael Gilday, Charles and Francois Hamelin, and Olivier Jean had been a strong medal contender.

[31] In the men's 1,000 heats, Ahn, 1,500 gold medalist, Charles Hamelin, of Canada and Celski of Federal Way, Wash., advanced to Thursday's quarterfinals.

[32] Ahn led all the way in his heat, provoking the loudest cheers from the home fans. Ahn gave his adopted country its first short track medal when he earned a bronze Monday in the 1,500. Sin Da-woon of South Korea, which Ahn represented in the 2002 and 2006 Olympics, won a photo finish for second in the same heat.

[33] Celski won his heat by a large margin.

[34] Hamelin, the world's top-ranked skater in the event, is trying to become the third skater to sweep the 1,000 and 1,500 at the same Olympics.

[35] Also advancing was Jean, Alvarez, Wu Dajing of China and Chris Creveling of Kintersville, Pa.

 **Answer the following questions.**

1. When and where did Li Jianrou win the gold metal?

2. How did Li Jianrou win the gold metal?

3. What is special about this final?

4. How did Li Jianrou think of this medal?

5. Who won the silver and bronze medals?

# Part B
# Reading

### Reading 1

## Brexit Wins: How Will British Sport Be Affected?[1]

*By Daniel Schofield and Cristina Criddle*

**Pre-reading Questions**

1. Are you a sports fun? And why?

2. Do you like sports? And why?

3. What kind of sports do you like most? And why?

4. What do you know about British sports?

*Your questions before reading the article:*

1. _____
2. _____
3. _____
4. _____
5. _____

---

1. Adopted from *Telegraph*, Jun. 24, 2016

Unit 4   Sports

*Words you know related to this topic:*
   **ball**

[1] Just about every area of British public life will be affected by the Leave vote. And sport in the United Kingdom will be no exception.

1. How will sports be affected by this vote?

[2] The freedom of movement principle allows sportsmen and women from the EU to ply their trade in the UK without needing a work permit that the majority of non-EU citizens require. This is particularly significant in relation to English football. Using the Home Office's current criteria for non-EU players, which require players to have played in a certain percentage of their national team's matches, more than 100 Premier League players would have failed to have gained a work permit.

2. What is their trade?

3. What are the current criteria for non-EU players?

[3] That would include players such as Dimitri Payet, N'Golo Kante and Anthony Martial, none of whom were established internationals when they joined the Premier League last summer. South American footballers such as Diego Costa and Philippe Coutinho have also been able to bypass the work permit process by gaining European citizenship before coming to England.

4. How could the South American players work in England?

[4] Before the Brexit result was known, leading football agent Jonathan Barnett told *The Daily Telegraph* that a vote for Brexit would compromise the competitiveness of the Premier League. "It is

5. How can the vote for Brexit compromise the competitiveness?

89

important that if we want the best league in the world then we remain in the EU," He said. Hence, it was little surprise that Richard Scudamore, the Premier League executive chairman together with all 20 Premier League clubs, came out in favour of Remain.

[5] As with much else in the Brexit debate, a lot of guesswork is involved in extrapolating the range and depth of the potential changes. All we know for certain is that the landscape will be different.

[6] "What will happen is that all our sporting bodies will have to sit down, look at all their rules and decide whether to emulate what they already have in relation to European nationals, i.e. give them preferential treatment, or do we fit the European nationals into the rules we currently have in the UK or do we want to write completely new rules?" Maria Patsalos, a Sports Immigration Partner at Mishcon de Reya LLP, said. "It is unlikely in football for instance that European nationals will have the same freedom as they have now if Britain votes to leave the EU."

[7] In that scenario, Premier League clubs could be forced to pay more as Dr. Babatunde Buraimo, a senior lecturer in sports economics at the University of Liverpool, argues. "Clubs will be limited to hiring higher-calibre players from highly Fifa-ranked EU countries," he said. "If the Premier League is limited to these players, this will increase the values, in terms of transfer fees and wages, of acquiring proven and established EU players. Missing out on rising talent [such as Kante] will be one of the drawbacks."

[8] However, as Patsalos makes clear, it is highly

6. Why should they stay in EU?
7. What do sports clubs vote for?

8. Why?

9. What was guessed about?

10. What is the difference?

11. Who are they?
12. What does the word "them" refer to?

13. Why should they pay more?

14. How will the values be increased?

unlikely those European players who are currently here, or who were signed during the negotiation period, will be forced to leave. "Historically the Home Office does not generally impose legislation retrospectively," Patsalos said.

[9] Yet there are some who believe that a Leave vote will enhance English football by curbing the number of foreign footballers in the top leagues. Introducing quotas for English footballers has long been a dream of various FA chairmen, but made impossible by EU law. "Whether they will be able to put that in place in the Premier League is probably unlikely but there is no reason why post Brexit they could not put nationality restrictions in say the FA Cup," Daniel Geey, a partner at sports law firm Sheridans, said.

[10] It is not just football that will be affected. Under the terms of the Cotonou Agreement and the Kolpak Ruling in 2003, sportsmen from Africa, Caribbean and Pacific Group of States (ACP) enjoy the same rights as EU players. This particularly applies to cricket and rugby union, where many players from South Africa, Caribbean and the Pacific Islands have come to play in the English domestic leagues.

[11] Several have gone to represent England. For 11 years between 2004 and 2015 encompassing 139 Tests, England started a match with a South African-born player in their team such as Andrew Strauss and Kevin Pietersen. The English rugby union team, too, has come to rely upon a large percentage of foreign-born players, from Mike Catt through to Manu Tuilagi.

15. Why will they not be forced to leave?

16. How can English football be enhanced?

17. What did the FA chairmen dream about?

18. Why was it a dream?

19. What will be changed after Brexit?

20. What other sports?

21. What is the Kolpak rule in 2003?

[12] Leaving the EU will render the Kolpak agreement void meaning future imports from such countries will count as foreign players. Again arguments can be put forward that this will encourage the development of homegrown players, but Christian Abt, a director at the Essentially sports management group, believes that the presence of more than 70 Kolpak players has enhanced the Premiership.

22. Then what will happen?

[13 "The Premiership will suffer as a result because it has such a cosmopolitan flavour to it which makes it so attractive to viewers and sponsors," Abt said. "As a product the best model is having international players playing alongside local and homegrown players."

23. Why did he think so?

[14] And what of London's status as the sporting capital of Europe, if not the world? It is the go-to destination for major sporting championships and for American sports looking to expand their audience. Although the NFL declined to comment, Patsalos believes Brexit will endanger the current London international series of games. "The way the NFL view it is that London is a gateway to Europe," Patsalos said. "My view is that (because) we pull out of Europe then they will reconsider that deal."

24. Then what will happen to London sports?

25. Why is it the go-to destination?

26. Why will Brexit endanger London Sports?

27. Who are they?

## Four players who would not qualify under the FA's criteria for non-EU players

Cristiano Ronaldo Signed alongside Eric Djemba-Djemba, David Bellion and Kleberson in the summer of 2003, Ronaldo had only just made his debut for Portugal as an 18-year-old.

**Thierry Henry** Although Henry had broken through into the French national team by the time he joined Arsenal from Juventus in 1999, he had not played enough games to have qualified for a work permit.

**David Ginola** Again his sporadic appearances for France would have precluded another dose of Gallic flair entering the Premier League.

**Dimitri Payet** The latest example of the Premier League's ability to create stars having been transformed from a bit-part player into France's leading player at the European Championships.

## Useful Expressions

| | |
|---|---|
| sporting bodies | 体育机构，体育组织 |
| preferential treatment | 优惠待遇 |
| higher-calibre players | 高水平运动员 |
| proven and established EU players | 已经成名的欧共体运动员 |
| rising talents | 新星 |
| render something void | 使某物无效 |

## Notes

1. The Leave vote (Para.1): 脱欧投票。Organized by "Vote Leave", the organization created in October 2015 and a cross-party campaign, including members of Parliament from Conservatives, Labour, and UKIP. This organization is

chaired by Labour MP Gisela Stuart, who also leads the Vote Leave Campaign Committee as Co-Convenor with Michael Gove MP. It successfully campaigned for the Leave vote in the United Kingdom European Union membership referendum, 2016. On 13 April 2016, Vote Leave was designated by the Electoral Commission as the official campaign in favour of leaving the European Union for the referendum on EU membership.

2. The freedom of movement principle allows sportsmen and women from the EU to ply their trade in the UK without needing a work permit that the majority of non-EU citizens require. (Para.2) 流动自由原则允许欧盟男女运动员不必申请劳工证就可以在英国球队踢球，而多数非欧盟国的运动员则必须有劳工证才行。本句中，现在分词短语 needing... 做介词 without 的宾语，that 引导的定语从句修饰 a work permit。

3. The Premier League (Para.4): 英超联赛。An English professional league for men's association football clubs and the country's primary football competition. Contested by 20 clubs members, it operates on a system of promotion and relegation with the Football League. Welsh clubs that compete in the English football league system can also qualify.

4. As with much else in the Brexit debate, a lot of guesswork is involved in extrapolating the range and depth of the potential changes. (Para.5) 有关脱欧虽然还有很多别的争论，但更多的是在推测脱欧可能带来的变化的深度和广度。

as with 和……一样，正如

5. "What will happen is that all our sporting bodies will have to sit down, look at all their rules and decide whether to emulate what they already have in relation to European nationals, i.e. Give them preferential treatment, or do we fit the European nationals into the rules we currently have in the UK or do we want to write completely new rules?" (Para.6) "有可能会发生的情况是，所有的体育机构将不得不坐下来，仔细审阅他们的规定，决定是否要仿照他们现有的对待欧洲球员的规定，如给他们优惠待遇，或者是否让欧洲球员来适合我们英国国内的规定，或者我们是否需要制定一些新规定？"

本句理解重点是人称代词：they、

them 和 we。搞清楚这些指代关系，就理解了句子的逻辑/纠正历史问题。

6. "Historically the Home Office does not generally impose legislation retrospectively," (Para.8) 有史以来，内政部都不会回顾性实施法律/纠正历史问题。

7. "Whether they will be able to put that in place in the Premier League is probably unlikely but there is no reason why post Brexit they could not put nationality restrictions in say the FA Cup,"... (Para.9) 他们想在英超实行英国球员配额可能实现不了，但脱欧后足总杯之类的不实行国籍限制是没有理由的。
本句中，whether引导的从句做主语。

8. Leaving the EU will render the Kolpak agreement void meaning future imports from such countries will count as foreign players. (Para.12) 脱离欧盟将使科尔帕克条款无效，意味着将来从这些国家引进的球员将被算作外籍球员。
本句中，现在分词短语Leaving...做主语，而现在分词短语meaning future...做状语，用于解释说明主句的结果。

 **Exercises**

### I. Reading Comprehension

***Finish the following tasks.***

1. Post Brexit, there will be differences for British sports in the following aspect:
   a. EU players will _____.
   b. Sports clubs will _____.
   c. British sports will _____.

2. According to Kolpak Ruling, the players of football, 1)_____ from EU, 2)_____ could play in British domestic leagues and represent Britain.

3. (T/F) The EU players need to get a work permit to play in British sports clubs either before or after the Leave vote.

4. (T/F) After the Leave vote, the English sporting bodies will not have any possibility to hire EU players.

5. The international sports will be happy about the change because _____.

## II. Vocabulary Development

***A. Please answer the questions according to the contexts.***

1. The freedom of movement principle allows sportsmen and women from the EU to ply their *trade* in the UK without needing a work permit that the majority of non-EU citizens require.
   → What is their trade?

2. All we know for certain is that the *landscape* will be different?
   → What will be different?

3. "… but there is no reason why post Brexit they could not put nationality restrictions in *say* the FA Cup,"
   → What does the word "say" mean here?

4. "My view is that (because) we pull out of Europe then they will reconsider *that deal.*"
   → What will NFL reconsider?

5. What do the italic words refer to in the following sentences?
   →1) *This* is particularly significant in relation to English football.
   →2) "Whether they will be able to put *that* in place in the Premier League is probably unlikely
   →3) *This* particularly applies to cricket and rugby union,
   →4) Again arguments can be put forward that *this* will encourage the development of homegrown players,

***B. Fill in the blanks with proper words.***

1. But as _____ many such suppositions in natural history, no one had ever tested it.
2. In the previous years of her marriage, she was limited _____ doing household chores.
3. The Namibia Hockey missed _____ on the World Cup ticket for 2016 after losing to a determined Zimbabwean team 2-1 in a highly entertaining semi-final.
4. I don't count _____ a good swimmer in our class.
5. Senator Smith worked on the other committee members to vote _____ the bill.

## III. From Reading to Speaking

Students can be asked to find information by themselves and prepare to introduce and comment on EU or Non-EU players who play in British sporting clubs.

# Reading Strategy

## 根据上下文确定词义

准确理解短文中主要词、短语及句子在特定语境中的具体含义或所指是阅读的关键，而除了查字典外，理解词汇更重要的是应学会通过上下文理解词义。

根据上下文确定词义通常使用的线索有：（1）标点符号如冒号、破折号、括号。这些符号的功能是说明和解释，也就是说，符号后面的内容是用来解释和说明符号前面的内容的；（2）词汇关系包括同义词、反义词、上下义词等。作者通常不会只使用同一个词语来描述一个主题，使用不同的词汇来进行描述一是为了使文章语言不单调，二是为了更加明了清楚地表达自己的思想。读者阅读时一定要注意前后句的词汇关系，它们通常有相互解释和说明的功能；（3）句子结构。作者使用一定的句子结构如从句（定语从句、同位语从句等）、排比句来准确阐述自己的思想，这种句子的功能通常也是用来解释一些抽象的、比较难理解的词语或概念；（4）功能为解释、说明的词语，如 simply put、that is to say、i.e.、this means that...、that is、put another way。这些短语经常作为插入语置于解释与被解释之间，而所引出的是个独立的句子，以解释前一个句子。

**例** Sleep experts say that most people would benefit from a good look at their sleep patterns. "My motto（座右铭）is 'Sleep defensively,'" says Mary Carskadon of Brown University. She says people need to carve out sufficient time to sleep, even if it means giving up other things. Sleep routines—like going to bed and getting up at the same time every day—are important.

"Sleep defensively" means that ____.
A. people should go to a doctor and have their problems diagnosed
B. people should exercise immediately before going to bed every night
C. people should sacrifice other things to get enough sleep if necessary
D. people should give up going to bed and getting up at the same time every day

**解析** 通常，文章的前后句都存在进一步说明、解释、阐述的关系，作者通过同义词、反义词等词汇关系表示出来。可以看出，选项 C 与文章有两组相对应的同义词。

**练习** Decide the meaning of the italics according to the contexts.

1. If the radiation does not hit anything important, the damage may not be *significant*.
   A. fatal      B. meaningful      C. remarkable      D. harmful
2. Hired troublemakers created *chaos* in the convention hall. Everything in the auditorium was in total confusion.
   A. trouble      B. complete disorder      C. noise      D. great excitement
3. It is better to be *reflective* about problems than to be thoughtless.
   A. thoughtful      B. considerate      C. calm      D. responsive
4. We couldn't get out but then as we don't manage to get out often anyway, that hardly mattered. We had local milk and eggs and when you buy your flour, beans, *lentils* and so on in 70lb sacks as we do, then you're better off than most people in towns. *Lentils* probably mean a kind of _____.
   A. spices      B. building materials      C. drinks      D. vegetable

Unit 4　Sports

　Reading 2

# Education the Heart of Olympics Says Rogge[1]

*By Nick Mulvenney*

[1] International Olympic Committee (IOC) president Jacques Rogge said on Sunday education remained at the heart of the Olympic movement with millions of Chinese youngsters now being introduced to its values.

[2] Rogge, who was opening the World Forum on Sport, Education and Culture in the host city of the 2008 Games, said the IOC had a duty to educate the world's youth on matters such as doping and even some not directly related to sport such as HIV prevention.

[3] "The goal of the Olympic movement is to contribute to building a peaceful and better world by educating youth through sport practiced in the spirit of Olympism," he told delegates to the three-day forum in the Chinese capital.

[4] "I am particularly pleased that this effort is being continued right now in China and that millions of young Chinese... are being introduced to the strength and power of the Olympic values such as friendship, excellence and respect."

[5] China returned to the Summer Games in

1. Why is education the heart of the Olympics?

2. What are the Olympic values?

3. QUESTION: _____

4. What is the Olympic spirit?

---

1. Adopted from *Reuters*, Oct. 22, 2006

1984 after 32 years outside the Olympic fold and Beijing organizers have invested heavily in education programs to spread the spirit of the movement to the youth of the world's most populous country.

5. Why does Beijing invest heavily in education programs?

[6] Beijing Organizing Committee (BOCOG) chief Liu Qi said the exposure of China to the rest of the world in 2008 would be an education in itself.

6. How can the exposure of China educate the youth?

[7] "Through the staging of the Olympic Games, we are willing to further reinforce the exchange with international friends and accelerate the development of China and Beijing to leave a precious legacy to China and world sports," he said.

## YOUNG PEOPLE

[8] Rogge said sport and the Olympics faced a battle for the attention of young people.

7. Why is it a battle?

[9] "We have to concentrate on this group who are today attracted by many other leisure activities such as music, video games, the Internet and movies," he said.

[10] "We have to maintain serious efforts to maintain their interest in sport and physical activities."

[11] He said warning athletes about the danger to their health caused by doping was a key element to the Olympic movement's education task. "Scientists and doctors who contribute to unethical behavior through the misuse of drugs must be stigmatized," he added. "That can be considered another form of education."

8. What is another form of education?

[12] The Belgian, who made his comments at the start of a week in which the International Olympic Committee (IOC) coordination commission will inspect Beijing's preparations for 2008, said he

had high hopes for the next Summer Games. "In conjunction with BOCOG, the IOC intend to make the Beijing Olympics a festival of harmony and peace, education and culture and above all of sporting perfection."

9. What kind of hopes?

## Useful Expressions

| | |
|---|---|
| at the heart of | 是……核心 |
| the host city of the 2008 Games | 2008年奥运会主办城市 |
| educate sb. on sth. | 教导；教育 |
| the spirit of Olympism | 奥林匹克精神 |
| be contributed to | 致力于…… |
| the exposure of China to the rest of the world/ showing China to the rest of the world | 向世界展示中国 |
| the Olympic fold | 奥林匹克团体/奥林匹克界 |
| leave a precious legacy to China | 为中国留下宝贵的遗产 |
| face a battle for the attention of young people | 为赢得年轻人的注意而努力 |
| warn sb. about the danger to their health | 警告某人其身体面临的危险 |
| contribute to unethical behaviors | 使得不道德行为成为可能 |
| have high hopes for... | 对……有很高的期望 |
| sporting perfection | 体育运动的完美 |

## Notes

1. 标题 Education the Heart of Olympics Says Rogge 的意思是 Education Is at the Heart of Olympics Says Rogge，报刊文章标题省略系动词。

2. ... education remained at the heart of Olympic movement with

millions of Chinese youngsters now being introduced to its values. (Para.1) ……随着成千上万的中国青年开始接触奥林匹克精神，教育就应该一直是奥林匹克运动的核心。

分词短语 now being introduced to its values 做定语，修饰 Chinese youngsters; its 指代 Olympic movement。

3. the World Forum on Sport Education and Culture (Para.2) 世界体育教育与文化论坛

4. ... the IOC had a duty to educate the world's youth on matters such as doping and even some not directly related to sport such as HIV prevention. (Para.2) ……国际奥委会有责任对世界年青一代进行有关兴奋剂，甚至一些与体育不直接相关的问题如艾滋病预防等的教育。

on 后面有两个宾语，matters... 和 some...。过去分词短语 not directly related to sport such as HIV prevention 做定语，修饰 some。

5. "The goal of the Olympic movement is to contribute to building a peaceful and better world by educating youth through sport practiced in the spirit of Olympism,"... (Para.3) 奥林匹克运动之目标应该致力于通过运动体现的奥林匹克精神教育年轻人，从而建设一个和平的更好的世界。"……

to be to do 用于表示 what must/should be done; by 表示建设的手段，through 表示教育的途径。过去分词短语 practiced in the spirit of Olympism 做定语，修饰 sport，相当于 which is practiced in the spirit of Olympism。

6. He said warning athletes about the danger to their health caused by doping was a key element to the Olympic movement's education task. (Para.11) 他说警告运动员服用兴奋剂对其身体有害是奥林匹克运动的主要教育任务之一。

现在分词短语 warning athletes about the danger to their health caused by doping 做主语，其中，过去分词短语 caused by doping 做定语，修饰 the danger。

7. That can be considered another form of education. (Para.11) 这可以说是另一种教育形式。

that 指代上一句 Scientists and doctors who contribute to unethical behavior through the misuse of drugs must be stigmatized,...

8. ... the IOC intend to make the Beijing Olympics a festival of harmony and peace, education and culture and above all of sporting perfection. (Para.12) ……国际奥委会想把北京奥运会办

Unit 4  Sports

成一个和谐与和平、教育与文化的盛会，尤其是一个体育运动的盛会。
and above all of sporting perfection = and above all a festival of sporting perfection

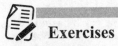 **Exercises**

### I. Reading Comprehension

*Answer the following questions briefly.*

1. What is the heart of the Olympics?
   _____

2. What other duties did the IOC have with the world youth through sports?
   _____

3. What is the goal of the Olympic movement?
   _____

4. How is the education of the heart of the Olympics going in China's preparation for the Games?
   _____

5. What does Beijing hope to reach from the Olympics?
   _____

6. Is it certain that young people in the world will pay much attention to the Olympic Games? Why?
   _____

7. What should the sports and the Olympics do about the young people in the world?
   _____

8. What did Rogge say about scientists and doctors?
   _____

9. What does the IOC intend to make the Beijing Olympics?
   _____

10. What is one of the key tasks to the Olympic movement's education?
    _____

## II. Vocabulary Development

### A. Answer the questions.

1. "The goal of the Olympic movement is to contribute to building a peaceful and better world by educating youth through sport practiced in the spirit of Olympism,"...
   → What kind of sports can educate the young people?

2. "I am particularly pleased that this effort is being continued right now in China and that millions of young Chinese..."
   → What kind of effort is being continued right now in China?

3. China returned to the Summer Games in 1984 after 32 years outside the Olympic fold...
   → What does the word "fold" mean here?

4. "Through the staging of the Olympic Games, we are willing to further reinforce the exchange with international friends and accelerate..."
   → How can we further reinforce the exchange with the international world?

### B. Fill in the blanks with proper words.

1. She never contributes _____ the discussion.
2. The best part of the job is her constant exposure _____ books.
3. Children need to be educated _____ the dangers of drug-taking.
4. There are 50 delegates _____ the conference.
5. He is our team's only hope _____ victory.

## III. From Reading to Speaking

The 2022 Olympic Winter Games was awarded to the Chinese capital Beijing. Suppose you are responsible for the event promotion, tell the class what you are going to do.

Unit 4  Sports

# Grudge Match[1]

Koreans and Japanese don't like each other much, so co-hosting the games has been a trial. But the countries' young are letting the old wounds mend.

*By Donald Macintyre & Hiroko Tashiro*

[1] Much is made of the healing power of sport—how simple games with unambiguous outcomes can modulate unhealthy rivalry and turn hatred into understanding. With that in mind, the World Cup's managing body assigned Japan and South Korea—two countries with a long history of mutual antipathy—to co-host the finals. This was supposed to encourage reconciliation. It was more like inviting porcupines to slam dance. Officials have wasted a lot of organizational energy arguing over inconsequential details, such as what to name the mascots, and reaching awkward compromises. There will be no joint opening and closing ceremonies, for example. Finding they have nothing in common to promote, officials resolved that the opener should showcase Korean culture, while the closing will be a Japan-only affair.

[2] Until recently, you could sum up the feud between the two countries like this: Koreans resent Japanese for subjugating and humiliating them during Japan's colonial occupation of the peninsula, which lasted from 1910 to 1945; Japanese consider Koreans to be louts and bumpkins, and moreover can't understand why bygones can't be bygones. The enmity has become ritualized. Whenever Japanese Prime Minister Junichiro Koizumi placates his country's ultra-conservatives by honoring war dead at Yasukuni Shrine, there is an angry protest from Koreans still smarting from atrocities visited on their country by war criminals. And then Koizumi makes the pilgrimage anyway.

[3] Yet, outside political and diplomatic circles where face is paramount, the gulf is being closed. The people of Japan and Korea—who are linguistically similar and ethnically

---

1. Adopted from *Time*, May 27, 2002

nearly identical—are experiencing a period of unprecedented cultural cross-pollination. A generation of young Japanese had discovered Korea's increasingly vibrant pop scene. Korean singer BoA outsold all Japanese artists in March. Instead of touring Europe, Japanese women these days are just as likely to visit Seoul to have a massage and shop.

[4] Meanwhile, Korea's youth, for whom the trendy present is more relevant than the remote past, sop up Japanese exports such as comic books, animated movies and video games. "The Japanese did us wrong in the past," says 20-year-old Lee Ho Yun as she sips a coffee at a Seoul café catering to Japanese manga and animé fans. "That doesn't mean we still have to hate Japan." During the occupation, Japan forced Koreans to take Japanese names, part of an attempt to stamp out Korean identity. Today Lee and her friends adopt Japanese nicknames for fun. She calls herself Izumi, because "it sounds pretty".

[5] The increased exchange can in part be ascribed to the easing of government barriers designed to prevent cultural "pollution". Korea banned imports of Japanese movies, music and other material until 1998. That year, Japan's then-Prime Minister Keizo Obuchi signed a written apology for subjugating Koreans, and Korea's President Kim Dae Jung agreed to a gradual lifting of the restrictions. Today most Japanese video games and movies can be imported legally. Game console software and songs with Japanese lyrics are still officially banned but are widely available.

[6] A stronger reason for cultural détente is Korea's newfound socioeconomic parity. Even Koreans will admit their lingering resentment is tinged with envy of a neighbor that seemed to be so impossibly rich and successful. But in the past several years, the peninsula has come up in the world. Korea's economy is soaring while Japan's stagnates. Korean companies that once copied Japanese electronic gadgets are growing fast and developing global brands. Samsung Electronics earned $2.1 billion last year, more than Sony and the other top five Japanese electronics makers combined. Korea had the best-performing stock market in the world in 2001. The country is a leader in its adoption of digital technology. At the end of 2001, more than half of Korea's households were using broadband, compared with less than 5% of Japan's, and the former's prowess at wireless communications rivals the latter's. "Korea is becoming more mature and confident as a nation and Japan is beginning to appreciate Korea for its achievements," says Lee Jung

Hoon, who teaches Japan-Korean relations at Yonsei University in Seoul. "The momentum is there for a much-improved relationship."

[7] Before, it was as if the cultural current flowed in only one direction, Japan to Korea. Today the polarity has been reversed. Now that they are being exposed to modern Korean aesthetics, Japanese are finding it harder to nurse stereotypes and prejudices. Recent Korean films such as *Shiri* (*Shuri* in Japanese) were huge hits in Japan. Korean stars regularly appear on television and K-pop is heard over the airwaves. Now that the poor cousin's fortunes are rising, it's O.K. to sample the cuisine. Japanese watch kimchi cooking programs and shop in specialty stores offering numerous brands of Korea's fiery pickles. Hosaka Yuji, an expert on Korea-Japan relations at Sejong University in Seoul, says, "Mass culture has taught Japanese things they weren't taught in the textbooks."

[8] Direct contact through tourism is also on the rise. Almost 2.4 million Japanese traveled to Korea in 2000, more than double the number of annual visits a decade ago. When she was in high school, Reina Ashibe thought Koreans were scary because they spoke so bluntly. A school trip to the country in 1998 changed that. When Ashibe arrived with 120 classmates at a high school in Seoul, they were welcomed with banners and loud cheering. Paired with a Korean student, Ashibe discovered her counterpart knew more about Japanese pop singers and movie stars than she did. The two ended up visiting an amusement park together and became friends. Now 21, Ashibe is so hooked on the place she's studying Korean history at Hitotsubashi University in Tokyo. "It was a nice big surprise that I could make friends there," she says. "When you actually meet them, they are very warm and kind."

[9] Still, relationships in general remain guarded. While nearly 70% of Japanese feel affinity for Korea, only 35% of Koreans say they have a warm spot for the Japanese, according to a poll by Japan's *Mainichi Shimbun* and Korea's *Chosun Ilbo*. Diplomatic rows seem certain to flare up regularly for the foreseeable future.

[10] Lee Jun Won, a member of a Seoul punk/ska band that features a Japanese trumpet player, says whenever their conversations turn to politics "there is always a little tension". The trumpeter, Jin Toshio, says he feels comfortable living and working in Seoul

nonetheless. When he goes drinking with his bandmates, he says, it's easy to find something in common. "With soccer and music," he says, "it isn't hard to make friends." Maybe there is something to the healing power of sport after all.

 **Useful Expressions**

| | |
|---|---|
| the World Cup's managing body | 世界杯组委会 |
| louts and bumpkins | 乡巴佬 |
| make the pilgrimage | 去朝圣 |
| political and diplomatic circles | 政治和外交圈 |
| unprecedented cultural cross-pollination | 前所未有的文化交流 |
| animated movies | 动画片 |
| stamp out one's identity | 消灭某人的特点 |
| sop up | 吸干，全盘接纳 |
| slick, sophisticated takes | 技法娴熟的、一次拍摄的电影镜头 |
| a gradual lifting of the restrictions | 逐步取消限制 |
| K-pop | Korean pop music 韩国流行音乐 |
| specialty stores | 专卖店 |
| feel affinity for sb. | 受某人吸引，喜欢某人 |
| have a warm spot for sb. | 喜欢某人 |
| the healing power of sport | 运动的治疗力 |

 **Notes**

1. It was more like inviting porcupines to slam dance. (Para.1) 这更像邀请豪猪跳拍手舞。 隐含意义是：It would make the two sides hurt each other./It was more like inviting conflicts. It

和上一句的 This 指代 assigned Japan and South Korea—two countries with a long history of mutual antipathy—to co-host the finals.

2. Officials have wasted a lot of organizational energy arguing over inconsequential details, such as what to name the mascots, and reaching awkward compromises. (Para.1)

and 连接两个 -ing 短语形式：arguing... 和 reaching...，做状语。

3. Finding they have nothing in common to promote, officials resolved that the opener should showcase Korean culture, while the closing will be a Japan-only affair. (Para.1)

分词短语 Finding... 做原因状语，主句中包含一个 that 引导的宾语从句，其中包含了一个 while 引导的状语从句。

4. ... why bygones can't be bygones (Para.2) ……为什么过去的事情不能让它过去

5. Whenever Japanese Prime Minister Junichiro Koizumi placates his country's ultra-conservatives by honoring war dead at Yasukuni Shrine, there is an angry protest from Koreans still smarting from atrocities visited on their country by war criminals. (Para.2) 每当日本首相小泉纯一郎去靖国神社膜拜战死的士兵，以安抚国内的极端保守者时，仍然因战争罪犯在他们的国家所犯的残暴行为感到痛心的韩国人总会愤怒地抗议。

介词短语 by honoring... 表示谓语 placate 的方式，分词短语 still smarting from... 做定语，修饰 Koreans，其中过去分词短语 visited on... 做定语，修饰 atrocities。

6. During the occupation, Japan forced Koreans to take Japanese names, part of an attempt to stamp out Korean identity. (Para.4)

part of... = which is a part of...，为非限制性定语，用以解释主句所陈述事实的目的或动机。

7. Now that the poor cousin's fortunes are rising, it's O.K. to sample the cuisine. (Para.7) 既然穷表亲开始富起来了，品尝一下他的食物也未尝不可。

the poor cousin 指 Korea。

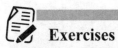

## Exercises

### I. Reading Comprehension

*Answer the following questions briefly.*

1. What's the purpose of Korea and Japan's co-hosting the World Cup?

2. How are the young people from Korea and Japan mending their old wounds?

3. Why have the Japanese always looked down upon the Koreans?

4. What's the major reason for the recent change of Japanese attitude toward Korea?

5. Why does the author mention the Seoul punk/ska band at the end of the article?

### II. Vocabulary Development

*A. Decide the meaning of the italics.*

1. Recent Korean films such as *Shiri* (*Shuri* in Japanese) were huge *hits* in Japan.
   A. blow　　　B. success　　　C. collision　　　D. impact
2. Now that they are being exposed to modern Korean aesthetics, Japanese are finding it harder to *nurse* stereotypes and prejudices.
   A. look after　　B. keep　　　C. give special attention to　　D. suck milk from
3. Now that the poor cousin's fortunes are rising, it's O.K. to *sample* the cuisine.
   A. taste　　　B. demonstrate　　C. use as a model　　　D. inspect
4. Lee Jun Won, a member of a Seoul punk/ska band that *features* a Japanese trumpet player, says whenever their conversations turn to politics "there is always a little tension".
   A. tells the story of　　　　　B. performs a role of
   C. gives prominence to　　　 D. produces a film of

*B. Fill in the blanks with proper words.*

1. The judge summed _____ the evidence presented.
2. The government is determined to stamp _____ crime.
3. You cannot always ascribe your failure _____ bad luck.
4. The parents worried about their child being hooked _____ playing games.

5. Her voice was tinged _____ regret.
6. The students felt that the school system had let them _____.

**III. From Reading to Speaking**

Do you know Ping-Pang diplomacy? Do you know any other sports diplomacy? Find the information and report to the class. At the end of your report, tell about your own views of this diplomacy.

Part C

Unit Assignments

1. Various sports, especially the Olympic games is the topic people like in daily life. Write an essay to discuss questions like (1) What can sports bring to us? (2) How can we value the achievements of the famous athletes? (3) What is the spirit of sports? Support your opinion with specific examples. And try to use the information and the languages from this unit.
2. List the questions you still have after reading these three articles.
3. List at least 10 expressions and sentence structures with meanings you have found in these three articles, and try to make your own sentences with them.

# Unit 5

# Global Development

# Part A
# Lead-in

# World Health Organisation Reports Dramatic Fall in Malaria Deaths[1]

Prevention measures including bednets and sprays help to bring deaths below half a million in previously vulnerable areas of sub-Saharan Africa, shows study.

*Reuters*

[1] The number of people killed by malaria dropped below half a million in the past year, reflecting significant progress against the mosquito-borne disease in areas of sub-Saharan Africa that were previously among the hardest-hit.

[2] The World Health Organisation's (WHO) annual malaria report showed deaths falling to 438,000 in 2015—down dramatically from 839,000 in 2000—and found a significant increase in the number of countries moving towards the elimination of malaria.

[3] The use of bednets, indoor and outdoor spraying and other malaria prevention measures have averted millions of deaths and saved millions of dollars in healthcare

---

1. Adopted from *Reuters, The Guardian*, Dec. 10, 2015

costs over the past 14 years in many African countries, the report said. Africa continues to bear the highest malaria burden of any global region, but death rates from the disease have fallen by 66% across all age groups since 2000, and by 71% among children under five.

[4] Margaret Chan, the WHO's director general, said the progress had been made possible "through the massive rollout" of effective prevention and treatment tools.

[5] "In sub-Saharan Africa, more than half of the population is now sleeping under insecticide-treated mosquito nets, compared to just 2% in 2000," she wrote in the report published on Tuesday.

[6] "A rapid expansion in diagnostic testing, and in the availability of antimalarial medicines, has allowed many more people to access timely and appropriate treatment."

[7] Two countries, Nigeria and the Democratic Republic of the Congo, accounted for more than 35% of global malaria deaths in 2015. Yet, the WHO said, an estimated 663m cases of malaria have been averted in sub-Saharan Africa since 2001 as a direct result of the scale-up of three key malaria control interventions: bednets, indoor spraying, and the use of malaria drugs known as artemisinin-based combination therapy. Mosquito nets have had the greatest impact, the organisation said.

[8] However, Pedro Alonso, director of the WHO's global malaria programme, cautioned that new challenges are emerging.

[9] "In many countries, progress is threatened by the rapid development and spread of mosquito resistance to insecticides. Drug resistance could also jeopardise recent gains in malaria control," he said.

[10] In the past five years, 60 of the 78 countries that monitor insecticide resistance have reported mosquito resistance to at least one insecticide used in nets and indoor spraying, the report found. Of these, 49 reported resistance to two or more classes of insecticide.

**Answer the following questions.**

1. How much has the number of malaria deaths fallen?
   _____

2. How were the malaria deaths reduced?
   _____

3. What has caused the malaria disease?
   _____

4. Which areas suffer malaria deaths most?
   _____

5. Are there any other problems that have not been solved?
   _____

# Part B
# Reading

## Who Owns You?[1]

A mock trial explores the intersection of patents and genetic-property rights.

*By Gary Stix*

### Pre-reading questions

1. Do you know who owns you?

2. Is gene related to human rights?

3. Do you know anything about genes?

4. Please list the rights you think you have.

*Your questions before reading the article:*

1. _____

2. _____

3. _____

4. _____

5. _____

---

1. Adopted from *Scientific American*, Mar. 24, 2002

*Words you know related to this topic:*
　　*mother*　　　　＿＿＿＿＿　　＿＿＿＿＿　　＿＿＿＿＿
＿＿＿＿＿　　＿＿＿＿＿　　＿＿＿＿＿　　＿＿＿＿＿
＿＿＿＿＿　　＿＿＿＿＿　　＿＿＿＿＿　　＿＿＿＿＿

[1] A man named Salvador Dolly gives blood for a routine genetic test to determine his fitness to father a child. The testing company, Advanced Genetic Testing Company (AGTC), then sells the remains of the sample to NuGenEra, a biotechnology company. NuGenEra discovers that Dolly's genes make him resistant to HIV.

[2] The company responds to this discovery by taking out a patent on both Dolly's genome and a series of gene sequences that confer resistance. When NuGenEra informs Dolly that his genes guard against the deadly virus, he decides to set up a business to market his blood to research institutions. To protect its patent, NuGenEra sues Dolly for patent infringement, saying that it owns his genome.

[3] Does the patent mean that Dolly must forgo any rights to his own genome? Does it violate his privacy or property rights? Should these rights be balanced against society's need for the tests and therapies for HIV that might be derived from NuGenEra's research on Dolly's genome? These issues were highlighted last November in a mock trial at the California Institute of Technology as part of the school's Program for Law and Technology, in collaboration with Loyola Law School.

1. What is the result of the test?

2. What does the company do with the discovery?

3. Then who on earth owns the gene?

4. QUESTION: _____?

[4] During arguments made by students from both schools, Judge Marilyn Hall Patel, who presided over the Napster copyright case, had to decide whether to invalidate the NuGenEra patent and throw out the company's suit against Dolly for violating the patent on his own genes. Many of the arguments centered on the usefulness of Dolly's genes—utility being one of the principal criteria for granting a patent. In its patent, NuGenEra claimed that both Dolly's entire genome and 10 genes within it, called the P sequences, could be employed to create diagnostic tests for determining resistance to HIV and to produce gene therapies to cure the disease.

[5] Dolly's attorneys argued that the genome—and even the P sequences—consisted of DNA for which the specific genes that conferred resistance had not yet been identified, a lack of utility that meant the patent should be declared invalid. They also contended that the patent violated Dolly's rights to privacy, property and personal autonomy.

[6] In her decision, Patel allowed the mock case to move forward to a jury trial. In doing so, she affirmed that the P sequences had a legitimate use as a diagnostic tool to ascertain HIV resistance. But she invalidated the part of NuGenEra's patent that covered Dolly's whole genome because of a lack of any clear-cut applications.

[7] Acknowledging an aversion to judge-made law, Patel would not embrace privacy or other public policy arguments made by Dolly's attorneys, citing the absence of legislation and case law to guide her. But she

5. QUESTION: _____?

6. So what about its usefulness?

7. What's the Judge's decision?

8. Why would Patel refuse the privacy argument?

did seem inclined to find some means of suggesting protection for genetic property within the bounds of existing law. The judge noted that genetic material is unique to each individual. Thus, Dolly may have the right to sue in California for misuse of his likeness for commercial purposes.

[8] The case illustrates how the genomics era may affect existing patent law. "I think that if this were a real opinion and it carried weight, it would mean that the patent laws are going to be aggressively pursued irrespective of these countervailing social policy issues," says Karl Manheim, who directs the law and technology program at Loyola. So if *NuGenEra v. Salvador Dolly* is any portent, whatever part of one's self that is locked up in the genetic code may be eligible to be owned and bottled by someone else.

9. How can the genomics era affect the patent law?

## Useful Expressions

| | |
|---|---|
| a routine genetic test | 一次常规基因测试 |
| make sb. resistant to sth. | 使某人对某物有抵抗力 |
| mock trial | 模拟审判 |
| take out a patent on sth. | 取得某物的专利权 |
| be balanced against society's need | 与社会需求通盘考虑 |
| throw out one's suit against... | 否决某人对……的起诉 |
| have a legitimate use as a diagnostic tool | 可作为诊断工具合法使用 |
| within the bounds of existing law | 在现有法律约束范围内 |
| the genomics era | 基因组时代 |

Unit 5　Global Development

## Notes

1. a routine genetic test to determine his fitness to father a child (Para.1) 确定他是否适合生孩子的一次常规基因测试
   不定式 to determine... 做目的状语

2. Should these rights be balanced against society's need for the tests and therapies for HIV that might be derived from NuGenEra's research on Dolly's genome? (Para.3) 社会需要从 NuGenEra 公司对多莉基因组的研究中获得检验和治疗艾滋病的方法，但某些（个人）权利是否应该和这些社会需求通盘考虑？
   介词短语 for... 做定语，修饰 need，其中包含 that 引导的定语从句，修饰 tests and therapies。

3. the Napster copyright case (Para.4): Napster 网站是 1999 年一位 19 岁的大学生创建的，它允许计算机用户通过个人计算机交换 MP3 文件，即 Napster 网站为网站用户提供软件。通过此软件，用户能够浏览本网站其他用户计算机内储存的音乐文件，并下载到自己的计算机里。2000 年，世界五大唱片公司起诉此网站侵犯他们的版权。五大公司胜诉，法院要求此网站立即停止交换由这五大公司出版的音乐及歌曲。

4. Many of the arguments centered on the usefulness of Dolly's genes—utility being one of the principal criteria for granting a patent. (Para.4) 多数争论围绕多莉的基因组的可用性展开——可用性是准予专利权的一项主要标准。破折号后面的部分是用来解释破折号前面的 center on the usefulness... 的原因

5. Dolly's attorneys argued that the genome—and even the P sequences—consisted of DNA for which the specific genes that conferred resistance had not yet been identified, a lack of utility that meant the patent should be declared invalid. (Para.5) 多莉的律师认为包含有抗体基因的基因组——甚至 P 序列，还未被识别出来，这也就意味着该基因组的不可用性，从而说明这个专利是无效的。本句为宾语从句，由 that 引导。从句中，过去分词短语 consisted of... 做定语，修饰 the genome，其中，which 引导的定语从句修饰 DNA，此定语从句中，that coroferred resistance 是 genes 的定语，后面又有一个同位语 a lack of utility that meant the patent should be declared invalid，其中又包含一个 that 引导的定语从句，修饰 a lack of utility。

6. "I think that if this were a real opinion and it carried weight, it would mean that the patent laws are going to be aggressively pursued irrespective of these countervailing social policy issues,"... (Para.8) "我想如果这一观点是真实而具有价值的话，那便意味着专利法将会受到猛烈的冲击，而不考虑那些相抵消的社会政策问题，……

本句含错综条件句，条件句中表述的是假设事实，与现在事实相反，从句中 that 所引导的宾语从句表述的则为真实情况。

7. *NuGenEra v. Salvador Dolly* (Para.8) NuGenEra 起诉 Salvador Dolly

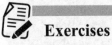

## Exercises

### I. Reading Comprehension

***Answer the following questions briefly.***

1. What does this article mainly talk about?
   _____

2. The main argument in the mock trial at the California Institute of Technology is about _____.

3. Why does the Judge refuse the privacy or other public policy arguments made by Dolly's attorneys?
   _____

4. Who owns Dolly's gene according to the mock trial?
   _____

5. What does the case of *NuGenEra v. Salvador Dolly* indicate?
   _____

### II. Vocabulary Development

***A. Try to answer the questions after each of the following sentences.***

1. The company responds to this discovery by taking out a patent on both Dolly's genome and a series of gene sequences that confer resistance.
   → "This discovery" refers to _____.

Unit 5  Global Development

2. He decides to set up a business to market his blood to research institutions.
   → The word "market" here means "_____".

3. To protect its patent, NuGenEra sues Dolly for patent infringement, saying that it owns his genome.
   → Who owns Dolly's genome according to the NuGenEra company?

4. Should these rights be balanced against society's need for the tests and therapies for HIV that might be derived from NuGenEra's research on Dolly's genome?
   → The word "against" means "_____".
   A. in opposition to          B. in preparation for
   C. into contact with         D. in contrast to

**B. Fill in the blanks with proper words.**

1. The researchers have been trying hard to find ways to guard _____ spreading infection of this deadly virus.
2. None of these social problems is unique _____ any country.
3. Schools are open to all irrespective _____ race, color, sex or creed.
4. The company entered a legal suit _____ the media.
5. He created a theory that derives speech _____ involuntary cries.

### III. From Reading to Speaking

Students can be divided into groups and debate on the following topic. There may be 4 students in each group. The students should make full use of the information and language from this article and try to find more examples from other sources to support their points.

**Topic:** Should the hospital or testing company sell the remains of blood samples to other companies?

# Reading Strategy

## 浏 览

　　浏览是报刊阅读的重要技能，它能帮助读者快速决定是否对所读文章感兴趣，以及该文是否值得一读。同时，快速浏览可使读者对文章主题有个大致了解，从而快速抓住文章主要论点。浏览报刊文章通常主要看以下几点：

* 大标题 (title)：文章中心思想的高度浓缩。
* 副标题 (subtitle)：对大标题的进一步解释和说明，所使用的语言较大标题更浅显易懂。
* 每部分的小标题 (little headlines/subheadings)：比较长的文章通常带有小标题，帮助读者注意所论述的一些具体的重要论点，同时帮助读者选择感兴趣的部分重点阅读。
* 每段的第一句 (the first sentence of each paragraph)：如没有小标题，每段的第一句通常充当主题句，阐明此段的主要论点。
* 插图、图表及其说明 (photographs, charts, graphs and the captions under them)：所有的插图和图表反映文章的主题，帮助读者决定是否对此文感兴趣。

**例** Still Can't Sleep?

—Need more sleep but can't get it? Here are some suggestions.

\* Stick to a regular sleep schedule.

\* Get regular vigorous exercise.

\* Watch your diet.

\* Be wary of sleeping pills.

\* Avoid stimulants near bedtime.

\* Limit late-evening alcohol.

\* Relax before bedtime.

\* Leave the lights off if you wake up in the middle of the night.

　Really can't sleep?

**解析**　假如你有个爱失眠的朋友,那么当你看到这个标题时便知道此文与睡眠有关,就会感兴趣。再读副标题,知道此文对怎样能睡个好觉有一些建议,便想知道有哪些建议(以便告诉朋友)。接下来浏览小标题(每部分的小标题总结了作者的建议),对文章的主要论点便有了比较清楚的了解。如果不想知道如何实施这些方法,便可就此结束阅读,然后去告诉朋友这些方法。如果想了解具体的做法,再去阅读全文。

**练习**　按照上面论述的阅读顺序,自己找一些报刊文章,浏览后试着叙述其主要论点。

# The Feelgood Factor[1]

Helping others to help yourself.

*By Philip Oltermann*

[1] When catastrophic floods hit Bangladesh last November, TNT's emergency-response team was ready. The logistics giant, with headquarters in Amsterdam, has 50 people on standby to intervene anywhere in the world at 48 hours' notice. This is part of a five-year-old partnership with the World Food Programme (WFP), the UN's agency that fights hunger. The team has attended to some two dozen emergencies, including the Asian tsunami in 2004. "We're just faster," says Ludo Oelrich, the director of TNT's "Moving the World" programme.

1. What's the job of TNT's emergency team?

[2] Emergency help is not TNT's only offering. Volunteers do stints around the world on secondment to WFP and staff are encouraged to raise money for the programme (They generated £2.5m last year). There is knowledge transfer, too: TNT recently improved the school-food supply chain in Liberia, increasing WFP's efficiency by 15%–20%, and plans to do the same in Congo.

2. What are the other offerings?

3. Why does the company do this?

## Balm for the soul

[3] Why does TNT do these things? "People feel this is a company that does more than take care of the bottom line," says Mr. Oelrich. "It's providing a

4. What is the bottom line?

---

1. Adopted from *The Economist*, Jan. 2008

soul to TNT." In a 2006 staff survey, 68% said the pro-bono activities made them prouder to work at the company. It also helps with recruitment: three out of four graduates who apply for jobs mention the WFP connection. Last year the company came top in the Dow Jones Sustainability Index.

[4] TNT's experience illustrates several trends in corporate philanthropy. First, collaboration is in, especially with NGOs. Companies try to pick partners with some relevance to their business. For TNT, the food programme is a good fit because hunger is in part a logistical problem. Standard Chartered, a bank, is working with the Bangladesh Rural Advancement Committee on microfinance and with other NGOs on a campaign to help 10m blind people.

[5] Coca-Cola has identified water conservation as critical to its future as the world's largest drinks company. Last June it announced an ambitious collaboration with WWF, a global environmental organization, to conserve seven major fresh-water river basins. It is also working with Greenpeace to eliminate carbon emissions from coolers and vending machines. The co-operation is strictly non-financial, but marks a change in out-look. "Ten years ago you couldn't get Coca-Cola and Greenpeace in the same room," says Neville Isdell, its CEO.

[6] Second, what used to be local community work is increasingly becoming global community work. In the mid-1990s nearly all IBM's philanthropic spending was in America; now 60% is outside. Part of this involves a corporate version of the peace

5. What else does it do?
6. What is providing a soul to TNT?
7. How does it help?

8. What trends?
9. How do they collaborate with NGOs?
10. Any example to this point?

11. What change?

12. Why?
13. What global work do they do?

corps: young staff get one-month assignments in the developing world to work on worthy projects. The idea is not only to make a difference on the ground, but also to develop managers who understand how the wider world works.

[7] Third, once a formal programme is in place, it becomes hard to stop. Indeed, it tends to grow, not least because employees are keen. In 1996 KPMG allowed its staff in Britain to spend two hours a month of their paid-for time on work for the community. Crucially for an accountancy firm, the work was given a time code. After a while it came to be seen as a business benefit. The programme has expanded to half a day a month and now adds up to 40,000 donated hours a year. And increasingly it is not only inputs that are being measured but outputs as well. Salesforce.com, a software firm, tries to measure the impact of its volunteer programmes, which involved 85% of its employees last year.

[8] All this has meant that straightforward cash donations have become less important. At IBM, in 1993 cash accounted for as much as 95% of total philanthropic giving; now it makes up only about 35%. But cash still matters. When Hank Paulson, now America's treasury secretary, was boss of Goldman Sachs, he was persuaded to raise the amount that the firm chipped in to boost employees' charitable donations. Now it is starting a philanthropy fund aiming for $1 billion to which the partners will be encouraged to contribute a share of their pay. No doubt that is good for the bank's soul.

14. Why and how does it tend to grow?

15. How much time is the work allowed?

16. What can companies benefit from the global charity work?

17. What are the inputs and outputs?

18. What does "all this" refer to?

19. But does cash still do?

Unit 5　Global Development

 **Useful Expressions**

| | |
|---|---|
| emergency-response team | 应急组织 |
| do stints around the world | 在世界各地工作一段时间 |
| emergency help | 紧急救援 |
| the pro-bono activities | 公益性活动 |
| a good fit | 最佳搭配 |
| a logistical problem | 物流问题 |
| water conservation | 水资源保护 |
| fresh-water river basins | 淡水河流域 |
| local/global community work | 地方 / 全球社区工作 |
| a corporate version of peace corps | 公司式的和平部队 |
| to make a difference on the ground | 在当地起一些作用 |

 **Notes**

1. TNT recently improved the school-food supply chain in Liberia, increasing WFP's efficiency by 15%-20%, and plans to do the same in Congo. (Para.2) TNT 最近改进了利比里亚的学校食品供应链，使得世界粮食项目效率提高了 15% 至 20%，并计划在刚果也要这样做。分词短语 increasing... 做结果状语，表示结果；and 连接两个时态不同的谓语 improved 和 plans。

2. ... three out of four graduates who apply for jobs mention the WFP connection. (Para.3) ……四分之三来应聘的毕业生都提到了公司与 WFP 的联系。

3. Coca-Cola has identified water conservation as critical to its future as the world's largest drinks company. (Para.5) 作为世界最大的饮料公司，可口可乐认为水资源保护对其未来至关重要。第一个 as 表 "看作"；第二个 as 表 "作为"。

4. Now it is starting a philanthropy

> fund aiming for $1 billion to which the partners will be encouraged to contribute a share of their pay. (Para.8) 现在它开始了一项慈善基金，目标是10亿美元，鼓励合作者们捐出自己收入的一部分。
> to 是和 contribute 搭配使用的，即 contribute a share of their pay to the fund。

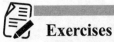

## Exercises

### I. Reading Comprehension

*Answer the following questions briefly.*

1. What does this article mainly talk about?

2. What benefits has TNT got from charity work?

3. What trends are there in corporate charity work?

4. Why was Coca-Cola mentioned in this article?

5. How do business companies go global through charity work?

6. How do employees feel about volunteer programs?

7. What do the new trends indicate about the charity work?

8. What does the author think about money donation now?

9. How can you help yourself by helping others?

10. What is the feelgood factor according to this article?

## II. Vocabulary Development

*A. Try to answer the questions after each of the following sentences.*

1. Staff are encouraged to raise money for the program.
   → The word "raise" here means _____.
   A. increase    B. collect    C. move upward    D. hold up

2. There is knowledge transfer, too: TNT recently improved the school-food supply chain in Liberia, increasing WFP's efficiency by 15%—20%, and plans to do the same in Congo.
   → The word "knowledge" here means _____.

3. Coca-Cola has identified water conservation as critical to its future as the world's largest drinks company.
   → The word "critical" here means _____.
   A. dangerous    B. very important    C. judgmental    D. disapproval

4. Part of this involves a corporate version of the peace corps: young staff get one-month assignments in the developing world to work on worthy projects.
   → Who are the members of the peace corps?

*B. Fill in the blanks with proper words.*

1. They all chip _____ for the benefit of the children in the quake zone.
2. The government worked in close collaboration _____ teachers on the new curriculum.
3. They have the soldiers _____ standby for any disasters.
4. What are you working _____ now?
5. All the arrangements are now _____ place for the opening of the Olympic Games.

## III. From Reading to Speaking

**TV talk show:** Two or three people form a group. Turn this article into a talk show. Suppose one of you is the host or TV presenter. The other or other two are the guests from TNT or NGOs or other companies mentioned in this article. The topic of the show is on "the corporate philanthropy". The task of the host is to ask questions and comment a little bit. The guests are to answer questions. Try to include all the information of the article with questions and answers. When performing, try your best to speak, making it a real show.

# Woman Challenges Tradition, Brings Change to Her Kenyan Village[1]

*By Audrey Schewe*

[1] When she was 14 years old, Kakenya Ntaiya entered the cow pen behind her home with an elderly woman carrying a rusty knife.

[2] As a crowd from her Maasai village looked on, Ntaiya sat down, lifted her skirt and opened her legs. The woman grabbed Ntaiya's most intimate body parts and, in just moments, cut them out.

[3] "It (was) really painful. I fainted," recalled Ntaiya, now 34. "You're not supposed to cry."

[4] For generations, this ceremony was a rite of passage for every Maasai girl, some as young as 10; soon afterward, they would marry and drop out of school.

[5] About 140 million girls and women worldwide have been affected by female genital mutilation, also known as female circumcision. The procedure is commonly based on religious and cultural beliefs, including efforts to prevent premarital sex and marital infidelity.

[6] While female circumcision and child marriage are now illegal in Kenya—new laws banning genital mutilation have contributed to a decline in the practice—officials acknowledge that they still go on, especially in rural tribal areas. Despite free primary education being mandated 10 years ago by the Kenyan government, educating girls is still not a priority for the Maasai culture. According to the Kenyan government, only 11% of Maasai girls in Kenya finish primary school.

[7] "It means the end of their dreams of whatever they want to become in life," Ntaiya said.

[8] But when Ntaiya endured the painful ritual in 1993, she had a plan. She negotiated a deal with her father, threatening to run away unless he promised she could finish high school

---

1. Adopted from *CNN*, Mar. 15, 2013

after the ceremony.

[9] "I really liked going to school," she said. "I knew that once I went through the cutting, I was going to be married off. And my dream of becoming a teacher was going to end."

[10] Dreams like Ntaiya's weren't the norm in Enoosaen, a small village in western Kenya. Engaged at age 5, Ntaiya spent her childhood learning the skills she would need to be a good Maasai wife. But her mother encouraged her children to strive for a better life, and Ntaiya heeded her advice, postponing the coming-of-age ritual as long as she could. When her father finally insisted, she took her stand.

[11] Ntaiya's bold move paid off. She excelled in high school and earned a college scholarship in the United States. Her community held a fundraiser to raise money for her airfare, and in exchange, she promised to return and help the village.

[12] Over the next decade, Ntaiya would earn her degree, a job at the United Nations and eventually a doctorate in education. But she never forgot the vow she made to village elders.

[13] In 2009, she opened the first primary school for girls in her village, the Kakenya Center for Excellence. Today, Ntaiya is helping more than 150 girls receive the education and opportunities that she had to sacrifice so much to attain.

[14] The Kakenya Center for Excellence started as a traditional day school, but now the students, who range from fourth to eighth grade, live at the school. This spares the girls from having to walk miles back and forth, which puts them at risk of being sexually assaulted, a common problem in rural African communities. It also ensures the girls don't spend all their free time doing household chores.

[15] "Now, they can focus on their studies—and on being kids," Ntaiya said. "It's the only way you can give a girl child a chance to excel."

[16] Students receive three meals a day as well as uniforms, books and tutoring. There are also extracurricular activities such as student council, debate and soccer. Class sizes are small—many schools in Kenya are extremely overcrowded—and the girls have more chances to participate. With these opportunities and the individual attention they receive, the girls are inspired to start dreaming big.

[17] "They want to become doctors,

pilots, lawyers," Ntaiya said. "It's exciting to see that."

[18] Just 4 years old, the school already ranks among the top in its district.

[19] "Fathers are now saying, 'My daughter could do better than my son,'" Ntaiya said.

[20] As a public school, the Kakenya Center for Excellence receives some financial support from the Kenyan government. But the majority of the school's expenses are paid for by Ntaiya's US-based nonprofit. While families are asked to contribute to cover the cost of the girls' meals, an expense that can be paid in maize or beans, Ntaiya covers the costs of any students who cannot pay.

[21] Each year, more than 100 girls apply for approximately 30 spots available in each new class. Parents who enroll their daughters must agree that they will not be subjected to genital mutilation or early marriage.

[22] Many families are willing to accept Ntaiya's terms, and that's the kind of change she was hoping to inspire. It took her years to drum up support for the project, but eventually she persuaded the village elders to donate land for the school.

[23] "It's still quite challenging to push for change. Men are in charge of everything," she said. "But nothing good comes on a silver plate. You have to fight hard."

[24] Chief John Naleke, a village elder, can testify firsthand to Ntaiya's powers of persuasion. As recently as 2006, he claimed there was no need for girls to be educated. But she managed to win him over; he's now an important partner in her efforts.

[25] Naleke said Ntaiya's accomplishments and spirit have made her a role model, noting that villagers also respect the fact that she didn't forget her promise.

[26] "We have several sons who have gone to the United States for school. Kakenya is the only one that I can think of that has come back to help us," Naleke said. "What she tells us, it touches us. ... She brought a school and a light and is trying to change old customs to help girls get a new, better life."

[27] In 2011, Ntaiya moved to Nairobi, Kenya's capital, with her husband and two young sons. She spends about half her time in Enoosaen, where she loves to visit with the girls and see them evolve.

[28] "When they start, they are so

timid," she said. "(Now) the confidence they have, it's just beyond words. It's the most beautiful thing."

[29] Her nonprofit also runs health and leadership camps that are open to all sixth-grade girls in the village and teach them about female circumcision, child marriage, teen pregnancy and HIV/AIDS.

[30] "We tell them about every right that they have, and we teach them how to speak up," Ntaiya said. "It's about empowering the girls."

[31] In the coming years, Ntaiya plans to expand her school to include lower grades. She also wants to provide tutoring for the students from her first class when they head to high school next year, and she wants to eventually open a career center for them. She hopes that one day the school will serve as a model for girls' education throughout Africa.

[32] Ultimately, Ntaiya wants girls to have the opportunity to go as far as their abilities will take them.

[33] "I came back so girls don't have to negotiate like I did to achieve their dreams," she said. "That's why I wake up every morning."

## Useful Expressions

| | |
|---|---|
| cow pen | 牛栏 |
| a rite of passage | （人生的）通过仪式，成长仪式 |
| to heed one's advice | 听从某人的建议 |
| to pay off | 使得益 |
| to push for change | 促进改变 |
| to be subjected to | 遭受 |
| to drum up support for | 竭力争取对……的支持 |
| beyond words | 无以言表 |
| a career center | 职业中心 |

**Notes**

1. While female circumcision and child marriage are now illegal in Kenya—new laws banning genital mutilation have contributed to a decline in the practice—officials acknowledge that they still go on, especially in rural tribal areas. (Para.6) 政府承认阴蒂切开术和童婚虽然是非法的，新的法律禁令也使其有所下降，但在肯尼亚，尤其是一些农村部落地区仍然存在。

    practice 和 they 共同指代 female circumcision 和 child marriage。

2. Despite free primary education being mandated 10 years ago by the Kenyan government, educating girls is still not a priority for the Maasai culture. (Para.6) 尽管肯尼亚政府10年前就强制实行免费的小学教育，Maasai 文化仍然不看重女孩子接受教育。

    分词短语 being mandated 10 years ago 做定语，修饰 free primary education。

3. She negotiated a deal with her father, threatening to run away unless he promised she could finish high school after the ceremony. (Para.8) 她跟她父亲达成了协议，威胁说如果他不答应让她在割礼仪式后上完高中她就逃走。

4. This spares the girls from having to walk miles back and forth, which puts them at risk of being sexually assaulted, a common problem in rural African communities. (Para.14) 这样女孩子们就不用为了上学每天来回走上几英里了，同时也就不再有受到性骚扰的危险。性骚扰在非洲农村是很普遍的问题。

    which 引导非限制性定语从句，说明前面整件事：having to walk miles back and forth 的结果或影响；a common problem 是 being sexually assaulted 的同位语。

 **Exercises**

### I. Reading Comprehension

*Answer the following questions briefly.*

1. What does the article talk about?

Unit 5   Global Development

2. What tradition did Kakenya Ntaiya challenge?
   _____

3. What change did Kakenya Ntaiya bring to her village?
   _____

4. How did Kakenya Ntaiya change her village?
   _____

5. How did the villagers respond to the change Kakenya has brought?
   _____

6. What made Kakenya achieve her goal of being educated?
   a. _____
   b. _____
   c. _____
   d. _____

7. To offer more help to girls, Kakenya Ntaiya is going to _____
   _____, _____ and _____
   _____.

8. The Kakeaya Center for Excellence, founded by 1)_____ in 2009, is a 2)_____ school of more than 3)_____ students in a 4)_____ village. It aims to provide 5)_____ and 6)_____ for Kenyan girls to realize 7)_____. It receives girls from 8)_____ grade. All the students can live at school which keeps the girls away from 9)_____ and the risk of 10)_____, and ensures them enough time to 11)_____. The school is 12)_____ by the Kenyan government and Ntaiya's US-based nonprofit. The students' families are asked to contribute to pay the students' 13)_____ in whatever way.

## II. Vocabulary Development

*A. Answer the questions after each of the following sentences according to the specific context being italicized.*

1. While female circumcision and child marriage are now illegal in Kenya—new laws banning genital mutilation have contributed to a decline in the *practice*—officials acknowledge that *they* still go on, especially in rural tribal areas.
   → What has been declined because of the new laws?
   → What still go on in rural areas?

2. Dreams like Ntaiya's weren't the *norm* in Enoosaen, a small village in western Kenya.
   → What is Ntaiya's dream?
   → What is the norm of Ntaiya's village?

3. Her community held a fundraiser to *raise* money for her airfare, ...
   → Who would pay her airfare to the US?

4. While families are asked to contribute to *cover* the cost of the girls' meals, an expense that can be paid in maize or beans, Ntaiya *covers* the costs of any students who cannot pay.
   → What does the word "cover" mean?
   A. hide          B. put a lid on          C. include          D. pay

5. Many families are willing to accept Ntaiya's *terms*, and that's the kind of change she was hoping to inspire.
   → What did these families accept?

6. She brought a school and a *light* and is trying to change old customs to help girls get a new, better life.
   → Paraphrase this sentence.

**B. Fill in the blanks with proper words.**

1. We only have two days to negotiate a deal _____ the overseas agent.
2. A more secure and peaceful world is what we should strive _____.
3. His hard working will eventually pay _____.
4. The hostages were subjected _____ extreme brutality.
5. If you keep disobeying the law, you are surely heading _____ trouble.

### III. From Reading to Speaking

   Suppose Kakenya Ntaiya was invited to our school to give a speech/talk/lecture. You were the presenter of the event. So at the beginning of the lecture, introduce Miss Ntaiya to the audience, based on the information from the article.

# Part C Unit Assignments

1. There exist many problems and issues around this world. Choose one of the social issues you are interested in, and try to write an essay to state your point of view about it and the solutions to the problems. Support your opinion with specific examples.
2. List the questions you still have after reading these three articles.
3. List at least 10 expressions and sentence structures with meanings you have found in these three articles, and try to make your own sentences with them.

# Unit 6
# Environment

# Part A
# Lead-in

## Climate Protesters Invade UK's Largest Opencast Coalmine[1]

Hundreds of activists take control of vast site and bring operations to a halt as part of a coordinated global direct action against fossil fuel companies.

*By Steven Morris*

[1] Hundreds of environmental activists have invaded the UK's largest opencast coalmine and halted operations across the vast site.

[2] Dressed in red boiler suits, groups of protesters crossed barbed wire fences to gain access to Ffos-y-fran mine near Merthyr Tydfil in south Wales. Some chained themselves to machinery, others lay across access roads.

[3] Dozens of protesters, joined by local people, also blockaded the entrance to the mine's headquarters.

[4] Hannah Smith, on site at the action, said, "Today we've shut down the UK's largest coalmine because we must keep fossil fuels in the ground to stop catastrophic

---

1. Adopted from *The Guardian*, May 3, 2016

climate change."

[5] Explaining the significance of the vivid red clothing the protesters wore, she said, "Continuing to dig up coal is a red line for the climate that we won't allow governments and corporations to cross. We are taking action in solidarity with the local community who have been battling Ffos-y-fran for nearly a decade, and now face the threat of a new mine next door."

[6] "Wales deserves a transition away from dirty coal, and the creation of sustainable employment in an economy that respects our planet and its inhabitants, now and in the future."

[7] The demonstration comes days before the Welsh assembly elections. Smith added, "With Wales going to the polls this Thursday and the climate crisis more urgent than ever, our action sends a bold signal that we must end coal now."

[8] Speaking from the heart of the mine, Sophie Stephens, a project manager from London, said the site felt "quite formidable" but said the atmosphere among protesters was good. She said some had played football and volleyball within the site. Workers had watched but not tried to step in as placards were strung between giant machines.

[9] Among the activists outside the HQ of mine operator Miller Argent was Coralie Datta, from Leeds, who said the idea was to stop traffic going in and out. "We're not setting out to be arrested—we're just going to have a party here."

[10] Andrew Dey and Maya Williams, from London, were there with their six-month-old son Robin. Williams said, "We're showing solidarity with the local community, who have to live with this mine." Dey said, "It's amazing to be here on a Welsh mountain but involved in a worldwide movement."

[11] Louise Graham, from north-east England, was handing out felt roses with environment-friendly messages tagged on to them. "I'm a mother of two and this is a way of being engaged in the very important job of protecting our world," she said.

[12] Retired coalminer Phil Duggan, who lives in the nearest village, Fochriw, said Ffos-y-Fan blighted the local community and plans to create another mine nearby had to be resisted. "This mine is killing the local area," he said.

[13] Natalie Bennett, leader of the Green Party of England and Wales, said, "If

we are to meet commitments made in Paris to keep temperature rise below 1.5℃ we need to end fossil fuel extraction now. The UK government is failing to act to cut our carbon emissions, instead it is decimating the renewables industry, pursuing fracking and continuing the operation of opencast mines; the UK's climate change and energy policies are in crisis."

[14] Miller Argent declined to talk to the Guardian. A spokesman told the BBC that the discussion around climate change needed to be "more balanced". He said the miners were proud of the job they did, which included supporting the steel industry.

[15] The company was given planning permission to mine the site in 2005 and has so far extracted more than 5m tonnes. It aims to extract up to 11m tonnes in all. It says it has created "high quality jobs" for more than 200 people—85% of whom live within 10 miles of the site. It has put forward plans to open a second mine nearby at Nant Llesg. Caerphilly county council rejected the application for the new mine but Miller Argent is seeking to overturn this decision.

 **Answer the following questions.**

1. Why did the climate protesters invade UK's largest opencast coalmine?

2. How did the coalmine respond to the protest?

3. Where is the coalmine?

4. Who are the protesters?

5. How did the protesters protest?

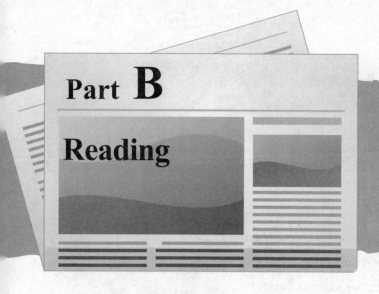

# Part B
# Reading

# How Do You Junk Your Computer[1]

A used PC can find life after death—but only if it comes out of the closet and goes to the recycler.

*By Anita Hamilton*

### Pre-reading Questions

1. What do you do with your used computer?
2. Can computers affect the environment? If yes, then how?
3. How can computers be recycled?
4. Why should we recycle the used computers?

*Your questions before reading the article:*

1. _____
2. _____
3. _____
4. _____
5. _____
6. _____

---

1. Adopted from *Time*, Apr. 2001

Words you know related to this topic:

_typing_ _____ _____ _____

_____ _____ _____ _____

_____ _____ _____

[1] In a cement-floored warehouse in upstate New York, half a dozen women sit hunched over computer work-stations. Holding a heat gun in one hand and metal tweezers in the other, they pry silicon chips from circuit boards like dentists extracting little metal teeth. Down the hall, a jumble of bright green motherboards spills out onto a conveyor belt headed toward a shredder that will rip them to cracker-size pieces of plastic. And around the corner, a clean-cut guy in a black work smock takes a big hammer and smashes one hard drive after another before tossing them into a huge bin marked ALUMINUM.

[2] No, this is not a PC factory gone berserk. This is the place where old computers go to die. IBM's Asset Recovery Center in Endicott, New York, is one of the largest PC junkyards in the world. Some 18 million kg of computers are dismantled here each year.

[3] It hardly makes a dent, however, in the annual bumper crop of dead computers. Every year an electronic trash heap nearly as tall as Mount Everest is tossed into garbage cans, stashed in garages or forgotten in closets. Some 500 million PCs will be rendered obsolete by 2007 in the US alone—abandoned by users who have upgraded to faster and sexier machines—according to a report by the

1. What are these people actually doing?

2. What will they do with the dismantled computers then?

3. What does "it" refer to?

4. How many dead computers are there every year?

5. Why are there so many obsolete PCs?

6. Then what should be done with these 500 million PCs?

National Safety Council. Computers are ranked as the nation's fastest-growing category of solid waste by the Environmental Protection Agency.

[4] And one of its most dangerous. Old PCs contain lead, cadmium, mercury and other unsavory components. Yet only 10% of the machines are recycled. Many of them find their way into landfills and incinerators, where they can threaten the environment. That's why the European Union has drafted rules that will hold manufacturers responsible for recycling their wares by 2008.

[5] To fend off similar legislation in the US, manufacturers are scrambling to devise recycling programs of their own—and hoping to make a buck while they're at it. Last November, IBM launched the first nationwide program; it charges computer users a $30 shipping-and-handling fee to take even an ancient PC off their hands. Hewlett-Packard is launching its own consumer-PC take-back program. Regional efforts—such as Sony's "recycling days" begun in Minnesota late last year—have sprung up from Oregon to New York.

[6] They face some consumer resistance. It's hard to pay a stranger to cart away a computer you bought for $2,000. Yet by the time you're ready to part with that machine, it's often so obsolete that no school or charity will take it. If you put it on the curb with the trash, however, it will end up in a landfill, where toxins could leach into the soil.

[7] A recycled PC, on the other hand, is literally a gold mine. Pentium and other processors have golden

7. Why are computers considered waste?

8. What about the other 90%?

9. Why can they threaten the environment?
10. And what can we do with them?

11. Do manufactures take any actions accordingly?
12. What are these programs?

13. How are these programs going?
14. Why do people resist?

15. Then what can be done?
16. Why is it a gold mine, and what kind?

tips. A computer's main circuit board, fashioned from copper and fiber glass, is studded with silver and gold connectors. A steel frame keeps the unit sturdy, and aluminum or copper heat sinks prevent the CPU from overheating. The outer plastic case can be recycled to make everything from pothole filler to pencil holders. Even the cords dangling from the back have rich copper wiring that can be reincarnated as pipes, pans or furniture.

[8] Yet for all the precious metals and other reusable parts, it's still tough to make any money recycling PCs. Minus the cost of processing, the average used system is worth a measly $6 in raw materials, according to electronics recycler Envirocycle in Hall-stead, Pennsylvania. The monitor is worth just $2.50. When IBM announced its consumer-PC recycling program late last year, it decided to have the carcasses shipped not to its 65,000-sq-m recycling center in Endicott (where it mines corporate PCs for parts) but to an independent recycler 50km away. The reason: "Typically all that low-end stuff is not profitable," says Lawrence Yehle, operations manager at IBM Endicott.

[9] So low is the material value of each PC that the first step in recycling is to try to resell the machine—either whole or for its working parts. IBM resells a third of the used equipment it gets back from corporate leases in online sales and auctions. "It's a profitable business for us," says Joe Lane, general manager for global financing. Old chips get second lives in electronic toys. Outdated CD-ROM and hard

17. Is it profitable to recycle the used computers?

18. Why is it hard to make money from this gold mine?

19. Then how can more money be made through used computers?

20. QUESTION: _____?

drives are reborn as replacement parts.

[10] When components are too old to be salvaged, IBM ships them to specialists in plastic, metals and glass. At Envirocycle, which does monitors, the plastic cases are popped open, the power cables chopped off and the circuit boards removed. Next the glass is crushed into pieces and stripped of various coatings so it can be sent to monitor makers that will re-form the rubble into new displays. MBA Polymers in Richmond, California, feeds whole keyboards and joysticks into its machines. The metals get siphoned off, then the plastic is melted into tiny pellets, which are resold for use in industrial flooring, auto parts and office supplies.

[11] Because metals are especially valuable, Hewlett-Packard mines its own. Step inside its 18,600-sq-m warehouse in Roseville, California (which it runs with partner Micro Metallics), and you will see computers stacked three stories high. A hulking blue machine swallows PCs and mainframes whole, grinds them up and a few minutes later spits them out in coin-size pieces. A system of magnets, screens and electrical currents separates out aluminum and steel, while the remaining mixed metals go to Noranda Inc., a copper smelter in Quebec. The metal scrap HP produces by the ton has a higher percentage of copper than ore excavated from the ground, according to Bob Sippel, Noranda's vice president of recycling. Last year the Roseville operation retrieved more than $5 million worth of gold, copper, silver, aluminum and steel.

[12] As recycling ramps up, computer manufacturers are discovering new ways to make the process more

21. QUESTION: _____?

22. How does it mine its own?

efficient. Metal screws are being replaced with snap-open panels for quicker dismantling. Lead solder used to fasten parts to circuit boards is giving way to safer tin, silver and copper alloys. Spray-on flame retardants, which can be toxic when recycled, are being replaced with metal paneling. And those annoying plastic shipping peanuts are being replaced with packing material made of water-soluble starch.

23. What do they do to be more efficient?

[13] Still, critics insist that more work needs to be done. "The efforts in the US have been chaotic and will not be successful until companies start picking up the excess costs," says activist Ted Smith of the Silicon Valley Toxics Coalition. In their defense, US manufacturers insist that government and consumers must share the responsibility—and the cost.

24. QUESTION: _____?

[14] "I can't go into people's houses and take their computers out for them," says Renee St. Denis, environmental-business-unit manager for HP. That's true. But if consumers aren't given sufficient incentive to turn their computers in, then all those recycling initiatives—not to mention all those PCs piling up in closets—could simply go to waste.

25. Why should they share the responsibility?

 **Useful Expressions**

| | |
|---|---|
| go berserk | 变狂怒，疯了 |
| make a dent | 引起注意，产生印象 |
| solid waste | 固体垃圾 |
| recycling program | 回收项目 |

Unit 6  Environment

| | |
|---|---|
| shipping-and-handling fees | 运输和处理费 |
| make a buck | 赚钱 |
| online sales and auctions | 网上销售和拍卖 |
| power cables | 电缆 |
| office supplies | 办公用品 |
| mine one's own | 充分利用自己的资源 |
| pick up the excess costs | 支付额外费用 |
| give way to | 让位于 |

 Notes

1. upstate (Para.1): northern (remote) parts of the state （远离大城市的）州的北部地区（边远地区）
2. Down the hall, a jumble of bright green motherboards spills out onto a conveyor belt headed toward a shredder that will rip them to cracker-size pieces of plastic. (Para.1) 大厅的另一端，一大堆鲜绿色的母板被倒到一条传送带上。这条传送带把这些母板送到一个粉碎机里，把它们粉碎成饼干大小的塑料块。
本句中，分词短语 headed toward a shredder 做定语，修饰 a conveyor belt；that 引导的定语从句修饰 shredder。
3. It hardly makes a dent, however, in the annual bumper crop of dead computers. (Para.3) 但与每年大量淘汰的计算机相比，这几乎引不起什么注意。
It 指代上段最后一句叙述的事情。
4. the Environmental Protection Agency (Para.3) 环境保护署
5. And one of its most dangerous. (Para.4) = And it is one of its most dangerous solid wastes.
It 指代上一段最后一句中的 computers。
6. So low is the material value of each PC that the first step in recycling is to try to resell... (Para.9) 正常语序应该是：The material value of each PC is so low that the first step in recycling is...；破折号后面是个选择句式，用以说明破折号前面的部分，即 how to

151

resell the machine。

7. MBA Polymers in Richmond, California (Para.10): 总部位于加州 Richmond 的 MBA 聚合体公司，其业务是将大批量塑料制品通过节能方式回收成为再生耐用品。

8. Lead solder used to fasten parts to circuit boards is giving way to safer tin, silver and copper alloys. (Para.12) 用来固定电路板上的零件的铅焊锡被换成了更安全的锡银铜合金。

过去分词短语 used to fasten parts to circuit boards 做定语，修饰 lead solder。

 **Exercises**

### I. Reading Comprehension

*Answer the following questions according to your understanding of the article. True/False items are indicated by a T/F before a statement. Some questions may have more than one correct answer. Others require an opinion. Choose the answer you like best in the space provided, give reasons for your answer.*

1. [T/F] Computers are thrown away when they cannot work.
2. Computers are considered harmful to the environment because _____.
3. [T/F] Unlike European manufacturers, US manufacturers resist to do any recycling programs because they cannot bring any profits for them.
4. Still, the experts are trying hard to make the recycling of computers a profitable business through
   a. _____
   b. _____
   c. _____
5. Manufacturers, government and consumers should share the responsibility and the cost of recycling the computers because _____.

## II. Vocabulary Development

**A. Paraphrases the italic parts to show that you understand their meaning. Try to do this practice without using a dictionary.**

1. Holding a heat gun in one hand and metal tweezers in the other, they *pry* silicon chips from circuit boards like dentists extracting little metal teeth.
2. Some 500 million PCs will be rendered obsolete by 2007 in the US alone—abandoned by users who have upgraded to faster and *sexier* machines...
3. Pentium and other processors have golden *tips*.
4. "The efforts in the US have been chaotic and will not be successful until companies start *picking up* the excess costs," ...

**B. Fill in the blanks with proper words.**

1. The children were already _____ the cornflakes when I entered the kitchen.
2. New buildings are springing _____ everywhere these two years.
3. He is willing to part _____ his right to vote.
4. To his own surprise, he ended _____ designing the whole car and putting it into production.
5. They are not going to give way _____ the boss.

## III. From Reading to Writing

**Survey:** Suppose you were invited to write a feature article about the effects of computers on environment for the campus newspaper. **First**, you should do a survey to collect some data to support your points. You can get the data from survey. The first question for your survey is:

*What do you do with your used computer?*

Based on the information you've got from the article "How Do You Junk Your Computer?" and other materials you've read before, design another 4 questions.

**Second**, you must ask at least 10 students and 5 teachers with these questions and take down their answers.

**Third**, sort out the data and analyze them.

**Lastly**, write your report, using these data to support your article.

# Reading Strategy

## 科学的阅读方法

我们在教学中发现，由于语言水平的局限，很多学生习惯于逐字逐句阅读，注意力通常集中在字和句上，尤其是那些自己不认识的词上，这从他们阅读时划出的词或短语就可以看出。然而划出这些生词实际上对理解文章毫无帮助。这也就是为什么多数外语学习者总觉得词汇量太小、读不懂、不知文章所云。我们通常的阅读目的是为了了解文章的中心议题，具体的阅读过程应该是：

了解中心思想→了解有关主题的不同观点→了解文章所持观点→作者如何论述（证实）自己的观点（也就是说，作者是如何说服读者的）

要完成这一过程并提高阅读速度，读者的注意力应该集中在以下3个方面：

* 每个段落的第1、2句和最后一句：要准确快速了解文章所提出的问题和所得的结论，达到阅读的主要目的，必须学会把握文章的主题句和主旨句。主旨句是陈述文章的中心议题及结论的句子，通常出现在文章第一段的第1、2句及最后一句和最后一段的第一句和最后一句。主题句是作者论述过程中的每个主要观点的核心句，通常出现在段落的开始或结尾。

* 已认识的词汇：试着把注意力集中到那些已经认识的词或短语上，你会发现这样即使不能理解所有的细节，你也能够理解文章的基本思想，了解文章的主要论点。当然，这一方法的前提是你已经掌握了大纲所要求的绝大多数词汇及语法规则。

* 关联词和副词：阅读的主要目的是为了获得信息，因此阅读时应该把注意力集中在文章脉络上，即作者所阐述的主题思想上，而不是对"只言片语"的理解。而关联词和副词则是把握文章脉络的主要线索之一。如作者在文章开始部分使用诸如but、however等转折词，通常是为了引出本文的主题。了解了转折词的这一功能，我们在阅读时就能很快地找到主题句或主旨句。

**例** Our bodies are wonderfully skillful at maintaining balance. When the temperature jumps, we sweat to cool down. When our blood pressure falls, our hearts pound to compensate. As it turns out, though, our natural state is not a steady one. Researchers are finding that everything from blood pressure to brain function varies rhythmically with the cycles of sun, moon and seasons. And their insights are yielding new strategies for keeping away such common killers as heart disease and cancer. Only one doctor in 20 has a good knowledge of the growing field of "chronotherapeutics", the strategic use of time (chroros) in medicine. But according to a new America Medical Association poll, three out of four are eager to change that. "The field is exploding," says Michael Smolensky. "Doctors used to look at us like, 'What spaceship did you guys get off of?' Now they're thirsty to know more."

**解析** 1）第1句提出观点，但How skillful？两个When引出两种具体的情况，说明身体如何保持平衡；2）第4句though转折副词引出相反的或不同的观点；3）第8句But转折连词引出与前一句相反的或不同的观点/事实；4）文中阴影部分为基本词汇，这些词汇已经足以使你了解文章大意了，剩下的生词或不熟悉的词汇无须在阅读过程中停下来专门去查字典，可留到阅读完毕后再去查阅。

**练习** 请根据上面建议的方法，用1~2句话总结下列段落的中心思想。

The college and universities of the 21st century will need to be able to work effectively in an interdependent society having a worldwide scope. They will be less inward looking and more connected to issues outside that involve problems plaguing society. They will be more collaborative with corporations, other universities and among faculty across units within the institution. There will be more emphasis on the student's experience in learning, seeking knowledge through different methods, in addition to the lecture, and developing skills through experience. Finally, the university will be more dependent on technology in the students learning experience as well as the operation of all aspects of the activities within the institution. I believe the University of the 21st Century will see students taking classes together and working on collaborative projects in universities that may be hundreds and possibly thousands of miles apart.

## Climate Change Lights the Touchpaper on Terror— We Must Fight Them Together[1]

Warming has been the ultimate "threat multiplier" in fragile countries, fuelling conflict and extremism. We must build resilience, and with it a climate of peace.

*By Harriet Lamb and Janani Vivekananda*

[1] In Paris this week, world leaders are working to agree a robust climate deal to curb greenhouse gas emissions. They are also grappling with how to tackle the pervasive threat of terror. The aim in both cases is to safeguard the right of current and future generations to live safe, secure and fulfilled lives. The fact that the climate conference is taking place in Paris grimly underscores this duality. But it isn't simply that tackling climate change and insecurity are parallel challenges. They are linked risks that need to be met with linked responses.

[2] Even if we get the best possible global agreement to cut emissions in Paris, the effects of warming already in the system will play out for at least the next two decades, with an impact on conflict, security and fragility. Climate change plays a role in the ongoing political conflicts in Darfur and Mali, and in food insecurity across the Sahel. Climate change has also complicated conflicts linked to the Arab spring, most notably in Syria.

[3] Of course, no conflict has a single cause.

1. Did the leaders achieve their goal?
2. What duality?
3. What are linked risks?
4. What kind of linked responses are needed?
5. Any evidence to show this impact?

1. Adopted from *The Guardian*, Dec. 9, 2015

Rather, climate change can exacerbate issues that can already cause conflict, such as unemployment, volatile food prices and political grievances, making them harder to manage and increasing the risk of political instability or violence.

[4] For example, Syria's 2006–2011 drought was the nail in the coffin, making fragile livelihoods of rural farmers untenable. With failing crop yields and falling incomes, many left to move to urban centres, such as Daraa, putting a strain on weak infrastructure and scant basic services. It wasn't the drought in itself that caused the conflict, but the existing social, political and economic tensions.

[5] The effects of climate change, such as more frequent hurricanes, long-term changes in rainfall and temperatures, and rising sea-levels are not experienced in isolation. They combine with social, political or economic factors already at play. In fragile contexts, where poverty, weak governance and conflict are frequent and the ability to cope with these risks is low, climate change increases the risk of violent conflict. Research conducted by International Alert for the G7 group of leading industrial economies found that climate change is the ultimate multiplier of threats.

[6] Climate change will continue to inhibit peace unless it is effectively integrated into managing risk and building resilience. Many of those most affected by climate change live in fragile states, where underdevelopment is intractable. The response to recent floods in the UK are unlikely to push local communities towards violence. Yet in the Indian state

6. How can climate change worsen the issues?
7. What kind of issues are they?

8. How can the drought be a deadly blow?

9. What caused the conflict in Syria?

10. Then what should be done to solve the problem?

of Tamil Nadu, the impact of devastating floods combined with poverty, endemic corruption and long-standing perceptions of marginalisation by Delhi have all created such tensions that failure by local or central government to respond adequately could pose a very real risk of violence or political instability. This will make it harder for affected communities to adapt to climate change and for authorities to provide adequate support in building resilience, locking them into a vicious cycle of conflict, poverty and climate vulnerability.

[7] There is much that can be done to ensure that climate change does not lead to increased conflict. Addressing the root causes of vulnerability to the effects of climate change—such as the lack of livelihood diversification, political marginalisation, unsustainable management of natural resources, weak or inflexible institutions and unfair policy processes—can help ensure countries plan for uncertainty and peacefully manage future risks.

[8] The best way to reduce the threat is to get the best possible deal at the talks in Paris. But with dramatic changes already under way, people need to adapt. And how people and governments adapt, especially in fragile contexts, is critical.

[9] Better policy responses are required to ensure that how we tackle climate change does not inadvertently fuel conflict. For example, a push towards renewable energy in 2007 saw a switch of land use from food production to growing crops for biofuels, which was perceived to contribute to higher food prices and resultant food riots in more than 40

11. Did the government take actions this way?

12. In what places will improper governmental responses to climate change cause insecurity?

13. Then what can be done to solve the problem?

14. What are the root causes?

15. Then how?

16. What will happen with improper responses?

countries around the world.

[10] If we want to reduce the risk of people falling into extremism through education, training and jobs, we need to make sure that those skills and jobs are "climate-proof". There would be little value in providing support for farming to unemployed young Syrians when long-term drought is the reason they cannot pursue a livelihood in farming.

17. What will happen with "not-climate-proof" jobs?

[11] Whatever happens in Paris, there will be new money for tackling climate change. If these resources address vulnerability, they could achieve the triple win of building resilience to climate change, conflict and poverty. Supporting the provision of sustainable livelihoods in Mali, buffering communities from the volatility of food prices in import-dependent countries like Yemen, and ensuring social safety nets are in place to protect the poorest when subsidies are removed in Egypt, will all address some of the root causes of conflict as well as vulnerability to climate impacts.

18. What is the vulnerability?
19. How can they achieve the triple win?

[12] We need leaders in Paris to agree a global deal to reduce emissions. We need adequate funds to support the poorest and most vulnerable to adapt. And we need to find ways for developing countries to progress in a low-carbon way. Single-sector interventions will not deal with compound risks. Integrating policies and responses in three sectors—climate change adaptation, development and humanitarian aid, and peace-building—is critical to ensure efforts on all three fronts can strengthen resilience to climate-conflict risks and create a climate of lasting peace.

**Useful Expressions**

| | |
|---|---|
| greenhouse gas emissions | 温室气体排放 |
| light the touchpaper on | 激发 |
| the nail in the coffin | 致命一击 |
| be perceived to contribute to | 被认为是导致……的罪魁祸首 |
| humanitarian aid | 人道主义援助 |
| a global deal | 全球协议 |

 **Notes**

1. Rather, climate change can exacerbate issues that can already cause conflict, such as unemployment, volatile food prices and political grievances, making them harder to manage and increasing the risk of political instability or violence. (Para.3) 然而，气候变化会加剧那些已经在引起矛盾的问题，如失业、不稳定的食品价格和政治动荡，从而使得这些矛盾更加难以解决，并增加了政治动荡或暴力的危险。

   rather 在本句中为副词，用以说明更具体的信息；that 引导定语从句，修饰前面的 issues；分词短语 making... and increasing... 做结果状语。

2. Better policy responses are required to ensure that how we tackle climate change does not inadvertently fuel conflict. (Para.9) 我们需要更好的政策以保证我们处理气候变化的措施不会不慎引起矛盾。

   本句包含 that 引导的宾语从句，其中又包含 how... 引导的主语从句。

3. For example, a push towards renewable energy in 2007 saw a switch of land use from food production to growing crops for biofuels, which was perceived to contribute to higher food prices and resultant food riots in more than 40 countries around the world. (Para.9) 例如，2007 年对再生能源的推行引起了土地使用的

变化，由种植粮食变成了种植生物燃料，这被认为是导致40多个国家高昂的食品价格和随之而发的食品骚乱的罪魁祸首。

which 引导非限制性定语从句，说明前面主句所描写情况的后果。

4. If we want to reduce the risk of people falling into extremism through education, training and jobs, we need to make sure that those skills and jobs are "climate-proof". (Para.10) 如果我们要降低人们通过教育、培训和工作变成极端分子的风险，我们就需要保证那些技能和工作是"抗气候"的。

people falling into... 为现在分词独立主格，做定语。

5. Supporting the provision of sustainable livelihoods in Mali, buffering communities from the volatility of food prices in import-dependent countries like Yemen, and ensuring social safety nets are in place to protect the poorest when subsidies are removed in Egypt, will all address some of the root causes of conflict as well as vulnerability to climate impacts. (Para.11) 为马里提供持续的谋生之道，减缓依赖进口的国家如也门的食品价格波动，并确保埃及在补贴被削减后的社会安全网络完善以保护最贫穷的人们。所有这些行动能够解决一些矛盾的根本因素，使其不易遭受气候影响。

本句中，三个并列的现在分词短语做主语。

6. Integrating policies and responses in three sectors—climate change adaptation, development and humanitarian aid, and peace-building—is critical to ensure efforts on all three fronts can strengthen resilience to climate-conflict risks and create a climate of lasting peace. (Para.12) 气候变化应对，发展与人道主义援助及创造和平三方的整合至关重要，它能够确保三方的努力能够加强对气候–冲突问题的应对，并创造一个持久的和平环境。

本句中，现在分词短语做主语，to ensure 后面是省略了 that 的宾语从句。

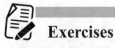 **Exercises**

## I. Reading Comprehension

*Finish the following sentences according to your understanding of the article.*

1. What is this article mainly about?

2. What kind of effects of climate change have we experienced in recent years?

3. What else can climate change cause apart from the climate issues?

4. How can climate change cause terror?

5. What should be done to solve the problems?

6. What was the main cause of the conflict in Syria?

7. Why was the push towards renewable energy in 2007 mentioned in Paragraph 9?

## II. Vocabulary Development

*A. Answer the questions according to the contexts.*

1. The aim in *both cases* is to safeguard the right of current and future generations to live safe, secure and fulfilled lives.
   → Whose aim is it?

2. Rather, climate change can exacerbate *issues* that can already cause conflict, such as unemployment, volatile food prices and political grievances, making them harder to manage and increasing the risk of political instability or violence.
   → What is the synonym of the word "issue"?

3. They combine with social, political or economic factors already *at play*.
   → What is the synonym of the phrase "at play"?

4. If *these resources* address vulnerability, they could achieve the triple win of building resilience to climate change, conflict and poverty.

→ What resources are they?

5. Integrating policies and responses in three sectors—climate change adaptation, development and humanitarian aid, and peace-building—is critical to ensure efforts on all *three fronts* can strengthen resilience to climate-conflict risks and create a climate of lasting peace.

→ Which three fronts?

**B. Fill in the blanks with proper words.**

1. Cesc Fabregas' tweet is met _____ angry responses from Tottenham fans.
2. Many investigators had grapple _____ the problem, usually with poor results.
3. We will have to see how the situation in my office plays _____ before we know whether we can take a vacation.
4. The unexpected epidemic put a strain _____ the resources of the hospital.
5. Are appropriate mechanisms _____ place to provide backup power for critical systems and facilities?

### III. From Reading to Speaking

There are researches about climate change and conflicts. What are the research findings about this relation? Summarize the findings and conclusions you've read about and then give your own points. Then make a presentation to the class.

# Reading 3

# A Tree Grows in Kenya[1]

Nobel Peace Prize winner Wangari Maathai long ago drew links between the environment and women's rights.

*By Alexandra Polier*

[1] No one was more surprised on Friday to hear from the Norwegian Nobel Committee than Wangari Maathai, Kenya's assistant minister for the environment. She was holding a meeting with her constituents near Mt. Kenya when she got the news that she had just become the first African woman to win the Nobel Peace Prize for her lifelong commitment to the environment, democracy and human rights. Maathai celebrated by planting a tree.

[2] In recognizing Maathai, the Nobel Committee is recognizing that Africa has been ignored for too long, and that the time had come to applaud the invaluable contribution of African women to their societies. Maathai, 64, has been Kenya's leading environmentalist for almost 30 years. She started the Green Belt Movement—an environmental landmark and human rights organization in Africa that has helped plant an estimated 30 million trees in a country now facing desertification, with only 2 percent forest cover remaining. While researching women's issues in the 1970s, Maathai found important links to the environment: malnutrition and lack of water, firewood and cash crops.

[3] "I don't see a distinction between environmentalism and feminism," she said in an interview at the Fairview Hotel in Nairobi shortly after accepting her award. "It's difficult for me to differentiate whether I'm campaigning as a woman or just as a human being trying to ensure everyone gets their rights." Maathai's plant-a-tree movement was the spark that ignited a feminist movement throughout Africa, giving women a sense of accomplishment and self-worth that

---

1. Adopted from *Newsweek*, Oct. 9, 2004

wasn't previously part of the culture.

[4] Maathai spent three decades fighting the system, and has now become part of it, using her role as assistant minister to achieve her goals from the inside. She has gone from persona non grata to national hero, and the irony of accepting the award Friday afternoon on the steps of State House next to President Mwai Kibaki was not lost on her. "For so long... just to be in Kenya was a problem [for me]," she said. "Now I am the government, I can influence decisions from the inside. Imagine that!"

[5] Maathai is no stranger to struggle or discrimination and has spent her whole life accomplishing what others told her was impossible. She was the first woman in East and Central Africa to earn a doctorate degree; first obtaining a degree in biological sciences from Mount St. Scholastica College in Atchison, Kans., in 1964. In 1966 she earned a master's from the University of Pittsburgh, and in 1971 received a Ph.D. from the University of Nairobi, where she taught for 16 years. It was there that she says she first experienced discrimination as a woman. "I started the campaign for human rights when my rights were violated as an academic at the university," Maathai said.

"They were treating me as an inferior because I was a woman and giving me less salary, although I was a very good teacher. The students said so."

[6] The second time she remembers being treated as a second-class citizen was by her husband, a member of parliament at the time, who divorced her in a highly publicized case in the 1980s because she was "too educated, too strong, too successful, too stubborn and too hard to control", it was reported. Maathai said the experience left her struggling financially as a single mother of three, and morally, as people began to judge her for having overstepped her place as a woman. It was a rude awakening that prompted her to start fighting back. "I wanted to demonstrate that as a woman you don't collapse because the world around you collapses. You keep going."

[7] Maathai did just that, spending the next two decades promoting the Green Belt Movement, which has produced income for 80,000 people in Kenya alone, inspired more than a million Kenyan children to plant trees on school grounds, and has spread to over 30 African countries, the United States and Haiti. Standing up for the environment put her in the line of fire of

the most powerful and dangerous men in Kenya but she did not flinch, and through years of persecution, imprisonment and beatings she persevered. "Moi gave us a lot of energy, he made us push harder," she said, remembering her strongest adversary, former President Daniel arap Moi. "We have made a difference. We have changed the political thinking in this country. We changed the way people think about the environment in this country." But when it comes to women's rights, she feels Kenya still has a long way to go. "I don't think women are treated equally, but we have better laws now than we had then. Today daughters can inherit from their parents, today we have a family court that protects children, and today domestic violence is more and more being looked at as a crime and not as something that must happen in the family."

[8] This isn't the first time Maathai has been recognized for her work. Over the years she has received numerous awards, including a listing on the United Nations Environment Program's Global 500 Hall of Fame. Klaus Toepfer, executive director of UNEP, said "Wangari has, through her passion, her intellect and her spiritual and cultural values, become one of the most important torch bearers for the environment, social justice and sustainable development. The Green Belt Movement has been an inspiration for thousands upon thousands of women both rich and poor, especially in Africa and developing countries. Wangari's fight against corruption and its cynical role in environmental degradation has earned her respect across Kenya, Africa and the world."

[9] On Friday, Maathai said she was overwhelmed. "Maybe after a night of sleep this will sink in," she said humbly. As for the $1.5 million prize, she said a good amount would go to a foundation for the Green Belt Movement to promote sustainable development, food security, soil and forest protection, and cultural conservation. "I'm sure my children have some ideas as well," she joked. As for her message to the youth of our world, Maathai encourages them to commit themselves to the common good. And, she suggested, plant a tree.

Unit 6  Environment

 **Useful Expressions**

| | |
|---|---|
| cash crops | 商品作物 |
| Green Belt Movement | 绿带运动 |
| persona non grata | 不受欢迎的人 |
| be lost on sb. | 未被某人理解/注意到 |
| a highly publicized case | 一个被深度报道的案子 |
| domestic violence | 家庭暴力 |
| put sb. in the line of fire of sb. | 使某人遭受某人的批评/攻击 |
| sustainable development | 可持续发展 |
| cultural conservation | 文化保护 |
| environmental degradation | 环境退化 |

 **Notes**

1. "It's difficult for me to differentiate whether I'm campaigning as a woman or just as a human being trying to ensure everyone gets their rights." (Para.3) "我很难说清楚我是作为一个女人还是一个为大家争取权利的人在战斗。"
分词短语 trying... 做定语，修饰 a human being。

2. ... and the irony of accepting the award Friday afternoon on the steps of State House next to President Mwai Kibaki was not lost on her. (Para.4) ……星期五下午在议会大楼的台阶上，站在总统 Mwai Kibaki 旁边接受这个奖是一种讽刺，而她也意识到了这一点。
be not lost on her 意为双重否定，文中接下来的句子用以解释这种讽刺。

3. "I wanted to demonstrate that as a woman you don't collapse because the world around you collapses..." (Para.6) "我要证明作为一个女人，你不会因为周围的人放弃就放弃……"

4. ..., which has produced income for 80,000 people in Kenya

> alone, inspired more than a million Kenyan children to plant trees on school grounds, and has spread to over 30 African countries, ... (Para.7) 此部分是非限制性定语从句，说明前面的 the Green Belt Movement，从句中有 3 个谓语：has produced、inspired、has spread。
>
> 5. Standing up for the environment put her in the line of fire of the most powerful and dangerous men in Kenya but... (Para.7) 支持环境使得她遭受到了肯尼亚最有权力、最危险人物的攻击和批评，但……
> 动名词短语 standing... 做主语。

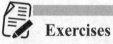

## Exercises

### I. Reading Comprehension

*Finish the following sentences according to your understanding of the article.*

1. This article is about _____.
2. Wangari Maathai won the Nobel Peace Prize because she _____.
3. Maathai celebrated the awarding by planting a tree because it is _____ that made her get the _____.
4. Maathai ignited the plant-a-tree movement because she found the important links between _____ and _____, _____ and _____.
5. The plant-a-tree movement is very important for _____ because it _____.
6. The plant-a-tree movement started in _____, and it has spread to _____, and inspired both _____ and _____ to plant trees.
7. Maathai started the movement after she experienced a) _____, and b) _____.
8. Maathai would spend the prize to promote _____, _____, _____, and _____.
9. The plant-a-tree movement is known as _____.

## II. Vocabulary Development

### A. Tell what the italics actually mean in the contexts.

1. In *recognizing* Maathai, the Nobel Committee is *recognizing* that Africa has been ignored for too long, ...
   A. know/see
   B. be aware/approve of
   C. approve of/be aware
   D. see/be aware

2. "I don't see a *distinction* between environmentalism and feminism,"...
   A. difference    B. excellence    C. outstanding    D. award

3. Maathai did just *that*, spending the next two decades promoting the Green Belt Movement, The word "that" refers to _____.

4. Standing up for the environment put her in the line of fire of the most powerful... men in Kenya but she did not *flinch*, and through years of persecution,... she persevered. The word "flinch" means _____.

### B. Fill in the blanks with proper words.

1. You must stand _____ for your rights.
2. His jokes were completely lost _____ most of his students.
3. The committee awarded her the prize for her long-standing commitment _____ the work.
4. They are campaigning _____ the house-owners to save the area from building development.
5. This put him _____ the line of fire of the whole class.

## III. From Reading to Speaking

Suppose Wangari Maathai was going to make a speech in our school. You are the chairman of the speech and are to introduce Maathai before her speech. Your introduction should be based on the information of this article only.

# Part C

# Unit Assignments

1. Write a 1000-word report to discuss the environmental problems in the near future. You can (1) choose one of the problems to elaborate, or (2) make an overview of the environmental problems. If you can support your article with data, it will be better, and don't forget to put forward some suggestions.
2. List the questions you have after reading these three articles.
3. List at least 10 expressions and sentence structures with meanings you have found in these three articles, and try to make your own sentences with them.

# Unit 7

# Politics

# Part A Lead-in

## UK Must Be Involved in EU Anti-terrorism Measures, Says Keith Vaz[1]

After recent events in Belgium, France and Germany, head of select committee says it is vital UK remains involved in security policies.

*By Toby Helm*

[1] Ministers must decide as a matter of urgency how to maintain maximum UK involvement in EU anti-terrorism, intelligence and security policies after recent events in Germany, France and Belgium, the chairman of the home affairs select committee has said.

[2] Labour MP Keith Vaz told the Observer he had written to the new home secretary, Amber Rudd, asking her to appear before the all-party committee because "after the Munich attack and other attacks across Europe, it is even more important that these relationships continue".

[3] Vaz said the committee would launch a major inquiry in September, as soon as parliament returned after the summer break, into the "Brexit implications" for security

---

1. Adopted from *The Guardian*, Jul. 23, 2016

and anti-terror policies.

[4] It would be vital, he added, that UK involvement in Europol and access to European criminal data bases, as well as participation in the European arrest warrant, continued until—and to as great a degree as possible, beyond—the time Britain left the EU.

[5] The prime minister, Theresa May, stressed in a speech before the referendum that the UK was safer as a member of the EU because of EU cooperation in tracking down terrorists and international criminals.

[6] On UK participation in the European arrest warrant, May said, "It has been used to get terror suspects out of the country and bring terrorists back here to face justice. In 2005, Hussain Osman—who tried to blow up the London underground on 21/7—was extradited from Italy using the arrest warrant in just 56 days. Before it existed, it took 10 long years to extradite Rachid Ramda, another terrorist, from Britain to France."

[7] But unless a special new arrangement can be forged, the UK participation will be weakened.

[8] In the same speech, May praised an EU directive which gives police and security services access to information held in other member states about the movements on flights of terrorists and organised criminals. "Most importantly, this agreement will make us all safer. But it also shows two advantages of remaining inside the EU. First, without the kind of institutional framework offered by the European Union, a complex agreement like this could not have been struck across the whole continent, because bilateral deals between every single member state would have been impossible to reach."

[9] Vaz said his immediate concern was that the UK had to opt in to a revised deal on how Europol, the EU's criminal intelligence agency, is run if it is to retain its involvement and keep key UK staff at its headquarters in The Hague, beyond May next year. The director of Europol, Rob Wainwright, is British.

[10] Vaz, who also warned before the referendum of serious security implications for the UK in the event of Brexit, said, "Theresa May knows how important this is but she put off a decision to opt back in to the new Europol structures as home secretary,

saying this could be done later. This is now urgent. If we do not opt in by January, the UK will cease to have any involvement and its staff will have to leave by May next year. Then we will have a weaker relationship even than the US, which has its own relationship with Europol."

[11] "After what has been happening across Europe, it is essential that we keep our counter-terrorism links with the EU."

[12] Rudd was a leading light on the remain side during the referendum campaign and will now have to negotiate with the UK's EU partners about the links a country outside the union can maintain.

[13] May added in her speech in April that the benefits were beyond question. "In the last year, we have been able to check the criminal records of foreign nationals more than 100,000 times. Checks such as these mean we have been able to deport more than 3,000 European nationals who posed a threat to the public. The police will soon be able to check DNA records for EU nationals in just 15 minutes. Under the old system it took 143 days."

[14] A government source said detailed discussion within government on how to proceed would be taking place in the coming weeks and months.

 **Answer the following questions.**

1. What must UK do according to the chairman of the home affairs select committee?

2. Under what kind of situation did the chairman say this?

3. What is the chairman's major concern?

4. What are the benefits for UK to keep involved in EU security policies?

5. What can keep UK involved in the EU security policies?

# Part B
# Reading

## Win-win Governance[1]

Now is the time for a more-cooperative world.

*By Dan Johnson*

**Pre-reading Questions**

1. What is globalization?
2. Can there be only one government in the world?
3. What is the responsibility for a government?
4. Can people with different cultures get along well?

*Your questions before reading the article:*

1. _____
2. _____
3. _____
4. _____
5. _____

---

1. Adopted from *The Futurist*, July—August, 2001

*Words you know related to this topic:*
**government**

[1] Globalization promises greater economic opportunity but also a host of complex problems. World leaders can have a positive influence on globalization by fostering an era of international cooperation, according to Michael Edwards of the Ford Foundation.

1. What opportunity and problems?

[2] "The changing global context makes cooperation both more necessary and more possible," writes Edwards in *Future Positive*, a study of how global cooperation might operate and what it means for the future.

2. How has global context changed?

[3] International cooperation surged at the end of World War II, when world leaders established the United Nations and found common ground on issues of trade, monetary systems, the mediation of conflict, and humanitarian aid. But during the Cold War many countries opted to intervene in the affairs of others, undermining the ideal of cooperation. The rise of democracy since 1989 and an increasingly globalized economy created the new connectedness within which governments and market forces now operate—and a greater imperative to cooperate.

3. What is the consequence of this option?

4. What is the greater imperative?

[4] "Either we pursue our own self-interest against a backdrop of growing inequality, insecurity, and degradation, or we embark on a new era of collective

Unit 7 Politics

action," argues Edwards, who directs the Ford Foundation's Governance and Civil Society Unit in New York.

[5] The continued well-being of countries could depend on a willingness to cooperate. Major powers might foster international dialogue in order to help manage a variety of problems that threaten their security and economic interests—including refugee flows, crime, terrorism, pollution, and the decline of natural resources. In this scenario, Edwards suggests that rich countries operating in a world of haves and have-nots will give aid aimed at "building capacities in poorer countries to find and implement solutions" as a vaccination against security threats.

[6] But international cooperation must be a true dialogue, not the one-sided imposition of the ideas of superpowers, Edwards argues. It must accommodate a diverse set of voices—including the alternative views of Islam, for example, along with the Western tradition—and create win-win opportunities for all countries. For Edwards, global dialogue and cooperation are nothing less than ideals that could "co-determine the future".

[7] Edwards's vision of global cooperation with all societies having an equal voice could be blocked if globalization has a homogenizing effect on the world's cultures. The wide gap between rich and poor also could compromise hope for meaningful collaboration, especially in countries such as Somalia, where unstable governments might not be capable of participating in a global dialogue. In other areas, ethno-nationalist movements have replaced undemocratic regimes,

5. Any advantages for both alternatives?

6. QUESTION: _____?

7. QUESTION: _____?

8. Can the ideals be realized?
9. What is Edward's vision?

rather than elected civil governments open to cooperation.

[8] In affluent countries, opponents of big government could undermine the political consensus necessary for international cooperation and push harder for free-market solutions. Edwards considers strong governments essential to global cooperation because they can contain the inequities of the market: "There is nothing more damaging to citizenship than social and economic exclusion. Letting imperfect markets loose in an already imperfect world simply produces more inequality, pollution, and alienation."

[9] With democracy growing around the world, global cooperation in the twenty-first century could get a boost from new governing alliances within a stronger civil society. Citizen groups, nongovernmental organizations, municipal governments, financial institutions, international organizations, and businesses are forming diverse and influential partnerships. These alliances have the potential to expand international dialogue and extend cooperative governance beyond the state-to-state model of the past.

[10] On balance, Edwards concludes that international cooperation is an obvious need. "The reality of increasing interconnectedness should make reciprocal relationships more acceptable to a skeptical constituency," he writes.

10. QUESTION: _____?

11. Who are the new governing alliances?

12. Why is it an obvious need?

# Unit 7  Politics

## Useful Expressions

| | |
|---|---|
| an era of international cooperation | 一个国际合作的时代 |
| the mediation of conflict | 争端的调和 |
| humanitarian aid | 人道主义援助 |
| market forces | 市场力量 |
| international dialogue | 国际对话 |
| refugee flows | 难民潮 |
| a homogenizing effect | 同化作用 |
| ethno-nationalist movements | 种族独立运动 |
| elected civil governments | 民选政府 |

## Notes

1. "Either we pursue our own self-interest against a backdrop of growing inequality, insecurity, and degradation, or we embark on a new era of collective action,"... (Para.4) 我们或者在不断增长的不平等、不安全和堕落的环境中追逐我们自己的利益，或者开创一个集体行动的新时代。either... or... 连接两个选择。
2. a world of haves and have-nots (Para.5) 富国与穷国的世界
3. push harder for free-market solutions (Para.8) 极力推崇自由市场道路
4. beyond the state-to-state model of the past (Para.9) 除了过去那种"国家—国家"模式外

 **Exercises**

## I. Reading comprehension

*Answer the following questions according to the article.*

1. Globalization can bring both _____.
2. The global cooperation will be destroyed if _____.
3. What is Edward's definition of globalization?
   _____.
4. There are some factors affecting Edward's global cooperation. They are
   a. _____;
   b. _____.
5. According to Edward, what is essential to global cooperation and why?
   _____.
6. The global cooperation in the 21st century differs from that of the past in that
   _____.

## II. Vocabulary Development

***A.*** *Try to answer the questions after each of the following sentences according to the contexts.*

1. The changing global context makes cooperation both more necessary and more possible.
   → The word "context" means _____.
   A. text         B. surroundings      C. situation      D. framework

2. The rise of democracy since 1989 and an increasingly globalized economy created the new connectedness within which governments and market forces now operate—and a greater imperative to cooperate.
   → What is a greater imperative to cooperate?

3. But international cooperation must be a true dialogue, not the one-sided imposition of the ideas of superpowers, Edwards argues. It must accommodate a diverse set of voices—including the alternative views of Islam, for example, along with the Western tradition—and create win-win opportunities for all countries.
   → The word "accommodate" means _____.
   A. consider      B. supply           C. serve          D. house

→ What kind of opportunities can international cooperation create for all countries?

4. The wide gap between rich and poor also could compromise hope for meaningful collaboration, especially in countries such as Somalia, where unstable governments might not be capable of participating in a global dialogue.

→ How could the wide gap between rich and poor countries affect collaboration?

**B. Fill in the blanks with proper words.**

1. The two countries are trying to find common ground _____ this issue.
2. The questionnaire aims _____ highlighting some of the major issues raised during the debate.
3. He has embarked _____ an adventure no one else has dared.
4. His words are nothing less _____ nonsense.
5. The policy leads to more rather _____ less involvement in a neighboring country's affairs.

### III. From Reading to Speaking

   **Pair work:** Peacekeeping by the United Nations is to help countries torn by conflict to create the conditions for lasting peace. China has sent peacekeeping forces to many countries under war. Work with your partner and make a list of countries the Chinese peacekeeping forces have been to. Then report to the class and tell the role these forces have played.

# Reading Strategy

## 语法和词汇手段

语法手段指作者根据语意使用相应的时态、语态、句子结构、连接词、指代词、标点符号等手段来表示句子与句子之间在结构上和语意上的关系，即句际关系（包括并列、对应、顺序、分解、分指、重复、转折、解释和因果 9 种关系）。作者通过使用各种语法手段把各个单句连成一个有逻辑的篇章，更加清楚地说明自己的观点。因此准确地理解句际关系能够更加明了语篇含义。通过句际关系，读者能够准确、快速地找到阐述主题思想的细节及根据，准确地做出推断，同时确定作者对所述话题持有的观点或立场。这里尤其要注意的是连接词和指示代词的功能意义。

词汇手段是指作者通过使用同义词、反义词、上义词、下义词、概括词或原词复现把语篇中的句子衔接起来，形成一个具有主题的语篇。通常论述一个主题的语篇所使用的词汇应该是同一语义场（semantic field）的。尽快地发现语篇中所使用词汇的相互关系是确定文章题材和体裁的关键，而迅速确定文章题材和体裁能够帮助读者迅速并较为准确地找到所读材料的主题思想。另外，确定同一语篇中词汇的相互关系还能够帮助读者确定某些生词，准确理解句子含义，领会作者的态度。

**例** Listen for Bush to strike three themes as the effort goes forward. He will evoke the coalition behind the war, signaling his attention to the concerns of other nations while clearly sounding a leader's trumpet. He will play his role as commander in chief of the home front, explaining the nature of the new conflict and trying to make clear how Americans' lives will and will not change. And he will—uncharacteristically for the son of a man who had to be urged to use the first-person pronoun—talk about his own personal commitment to the cause. "I will not forget the wound to our country and those who inflicted it," he said in September. "I will not yield. I will not rest." Either in the war on terror—or the war of words.

**解析**  1) 用句子表示列举：3 个平行结构：He will... He will... And he will...

2) 分词短语解释主句内容：signaling... 和 explaining...

3) 同语义场词汇表示文章主题：war, conflict, the cause, the front, the commander in chief, the wound

**练习**  参照例句分析下列段落所使用的语法词汇手段。

Sea-level rise as a consequence of global warming would immediately threaten that large fraction of the globe living at sea level. Nearly one-third of all human beings live within 36 miles of a coastline. Most of the world's great sea-port cities would be endangered: New Orleans, Amsterdam, Shanghai, Cairo. Some countries—Maldives Islands in the Indian Ocean, islands in the Pacific—would be inundated. Heavily populated coastal areas such as in Bangladesh and Egypt, where large populations occupy low-lying areas, would suffer extreme dislocation.

# The New Words of War[1]

Never entirely at home with the English language, Bush is redefining the vocabulary of conflict.

*By Jon Meacham*

[1] It was not the role he expected to play. "My father was the last president of a great generation," George W. Bush said in the summer of 2000. "A generation of Americans who stormed beaches, liberated concentration camps and delivered us from evil... Now the question comes to the sons and daughters of this achievement: what is asked of us?" The answer was not about war or terror. "Never has the promise of prosperity been so vivid," Bush went on, somewhat defensively adding, "But times of plenty, like times of crisis, are tests of American character."

[2] Now he has a crisis of historic dimension, and a boomer politician who was expected to spend his White House years managing a budget surplus is a war president with a difficult brief: he must simultaneously fight and define a war with no clear precedent in American history. It is a rhetorical task that would have challenged even Franklin Roosevelt and Ronald Reagan, neither of whom had the kind of on-again, off-again relationship that Bush has with the English language. Yet George Bush is creating a new vocabulary of war, one that evokes urgency while

1. What role is he playing now?
2. And what role does he expect to play?

3. What is the question?

4. What is the answer?

5. QUESTION: _____?
6. Why a boomer politician?

7. What difficult brief?

8. What is the task?

---

1. Adopted from *Newsweek Special Issue*, 2002

calling for open-ended patience.

[3] It is a complicated job. American wars have usually been about defeating specific enemies, toppling particular capitals, and then moving on. Appeals for the public to stay the course generally center on sacrifices "for the duration"—often a period of years, but ordinarily not for an indefinite, generations-long sprawl. This is a very special kind of conflict, one that will not end with a VE or VJ Day. Bush—and his successors—must find a way to talk about the war that keeps Americans engaged but not exhausted. There is little more perishable than the drama of a conflict's opening hours.

[4] Impatience is a real risk. The rhetoric of combat is now a national commonplace: the word connotes urgency, clarity and energy, and thus presidents have tried to rally support by declaring "war" on a variety of nonmilitary scourges. Eisenhower was the first to use the term in this unconventional sense, calling for a war on hunger; LBJ's war on poverty shaped the 60's. So, where once we had only wars against foreign powers, we have grown accustomed in recent years to different kinds of open-ended "wars" at home, against cancer, crime and illegal drugs. Worthy targets all, but by nature poverty and crime and drugs are more elusive quarry than, say, Berlin, Rome and Tokyo were in the 1940s—and the word "war" itself is more familiar, and therefore potentially less powerful, than it once was. Bush realizes this. "Americans should not expect one battle, but a lengthy campaign unlike any other we have ever seen," the president told

9. QUESTION: _____ ?

10. How long is "the duration" ?

11. Why is that a special kind?

12. What kind of nonmilitary disasters?

Congress after September 11.

[5] For all the seeming parallels with World War II—the popular Rooseveltian evocation of September 11 as a "date which will live in infamy"; the Churchillian echoes in Bush's pledge that "we will not tire, we will not falter and we will not fail"—this conflict's language is being drawn, directly and indirectly, from both the fight against the Axis and the cold war. "This does not fit neatly into any one historical category," says Bush speechwriter Michael Gerson. "We have a cold war that was begun by a Pearl Harbor."

[6] The closest thing to a template for the first war of the 21st century may lie near the end of one of the most remarkable Inaugural Addresses of the 20th: John F. Kennedy's. "Now the trumpet summons us again," the young president said on Jan. 20, 1961, "not as a call to bear arms, though arms we need; not as a call to battle, though embattled we are—but a call to bear the burden of a long twilight struggle, year in and year out..."

[7] A long twilight struggle. Asked about the image 40 years later, Ted Sorensen, the Kennedy adviser and a key architect of the JFK speech, says, "It's a perfectly appropriate phrase for a war that's not out in the open, the enemy's not out in the open, the tactics are not out in the open. In 1961 the point was to differentiate the cold war from a conventional war, which was between two governments or coalitions of governments unfolding primarily on a battlefield. That was not true in the cold war."

[8] And it is not entirely true in the war against terrorism. This battle, will take many forms, from

13. What seeming similarities?

14. What does "Pearl Harbor" here represent?

15. Which war is the first war of the 21st century?

16. What does "a long twilight struggle" mean?

the clash of arms in a proxy place (Afghanistan now, Vietnam then) to a constant habit of mind.

[9] Listen for Bush to strike three themes as the effort goes forward. He will evoke the coalition behind the war, signaling his attention to the concerns of other nations while clearly sounding a leader's trumpet. He will play his role as commander in chief of the home front, explaining the nature of the new conflict and trying to make clear how Americans' lives will and will not change. And he will—uncharacteristically for the son of a man who had to be urged to use the first-person pronoun—talk about his own personal commitment to the cause. "I will not forget the wound to our country and those who inflicted it," he said in September. "I will not yield. I will not rest." Either in the war on terror—or the war of words.

17. QUESTION:_____?

 **Useful Expressions**

| | |
|---|---|
| American character | 美国性格 |
| a boomer politician | 一个繁荣时期的政治家 |
| a budget surplus | 预算赤字 |
| on-again, off-again relationship | 飘忽不定 / 不确定的关系 |
| stay the course | 贯彻始终，坚持到底 |
| nonmilitary scourges | 非军事灾难 |
| by nature | 本质上 |
| the cold war | 冷战 |
| a conventional war | 常规战 |
| sound a leader's trumpet | 吹响领导者的号角 |
| one's own personal commitment | 某人的个人事业 |

# Notes

1. **A generation of Americans who stormed beaches, liberated concentration camps and delivered us from evil...** (Para.1) 本句指第二次世界大战时期的一代人。stormed beaches 描述欧洲战场，liberated concentration camps 描述德国战场，delivered us from evil 则是描述击败日本。

2. **It is a rhetorical task that would have challenged even Franklin Roosevelt and Ronald Reagan, neither of whom had the kind of on-again, off-again relationship that Bush has with the English language.** (Para.2) 这是一个能将富兰克林·罗斯福和罗纳德·里根难住的语言文字任务，布什这种和英语语言飘忽不定的关系他们两个谁都没有遇到过。neither of whom... 非限制性定语从句，用于解释为什么被难住。

3. **Appeals for the public to stay the course generally center on sacrifices "for the duration"—often a period of years, but ordinarily not for an indefinite, generations-long sprawl.** (Para.3) 要求公众坚持到底通常是要大家做出"时间"上的牺牲——这个时间通常是几年，但一般不会是不确定的、几代人那么长。破折号后面用以解释 duration，即时间的长度。

4. **VE (Para.3):** Victory in Europe（第二次世界大战中）欧洲胜利日
   **VJ Day (Para.3):** Victory over Japan Day（第二次世界大战中）抗战胜利日

5. **There is little more perishable than the drama of a conflict's opening hours.** (Para.3) 没有什么比战争开始那几个小时的戏剧性更易于消失了。
   本句为比较级结构，其中，little 为名词，形容词短语 more perishable than the drama of a conflict's opening hours 修饰 little。

6. **LBJ (Para.4):** Lydon Baines Johnson 美国第36任总统（1963—1969）。

7. **Worthy targets all, but by nature poverty and crime and drugs are more elusive quarry than, say, Berlin, Rome and Tokyo were in the 1940s...** (Para.4) Worthy targets all 为本句主语。由 but 引出的 by nature poverty and crime and drugs 是 Worthy targets all 的同位语。

8. **a "date which will live in infamy"** (Para.5) 一个将被作为耻辱日传诸后世的日子

9. **the Axis (Para.5):** 轴心国，第二次世界大战中德、意、日三国联盟

Unit 7  Politics

10. We have a cold war that was begun by a Pearl Harbor. (Para.5) 我们现在正经历着一次由珍珠港引发的冷战。
11. This battle will take many forms, from the clash of arms in a proxy place (Afghanistan now, Vietnam then) to a constant habit of mind. (Para.8)
    proxy war 代理战争，傀儡战争（由大国挑动或操纵的一定规模或一定范围的战争）
12. Either in the war on terror— or the war of words. (Para.9) = I will not yield, and will not rest either in the war on terror, or in the war of words. (words = vocabulary to describe war)

 **Exercises**

**I. Reading Comprehension**

*Answer the following questions briefly.*

1. What was the role Bush expected to play before September 11?

2. What is the role Bush actually playing now?

3. What have the American wars usually been about?

4. What is the war this time like?

5. In what way should Bush talk about the war?

6. What is the author's attitude toward the war between America and Afghanistan?

**II. Vocabulary Development**

*A. Answer the questions after each of the following sentences with the context clues.*

1. "A generation of Americans who stormed beaches, liberated concentration camps and delivered us from evil... Now the question comes to the sons and daughters of this achievement: what is asked of us?"

→ What does "this achievement" refer to?

2. Yet George Bush is creating a new vocabulary of war, one that evokes urgency while calling for open-ended patience.
   → How should Bush describe "war"?

3. Worthy targets all, but by nature poverty and crime and drugs are more elusive quarry than, say, Berlin, Rome and Tokyo were in the 1940s...
   → What are the worthy targets?

4. ... and the word "war" itself is more familiar, and therefore potentially less powerful, than it once was. Bush realizes this. "Americans should not expect one battle, but a lengthy campaign unlike any other we have ever seen," the president told Congress after September 11.
   → Why is the word "war" less powerful than it once was?
   → The word "this" refers to _____.

5. ..., the Kennedy adviser and a key architect of the JFK speech, says, ...
   → The word "architect" means _____.

**B. Fill in the blanks with proper words.**

1. The mayor launched an appeal _____ the public to give blood to the victims of the disaster.
2. Their thoughts center _____ one idea.
3. When the American government wants to fight abroad, it would declare wars _____ nonmilitary targets at home.
4. The newcomers have to try hard to fit _____ their new surroundings.
5. The speaker drew attention _____ the point at issue.

### III. From Reading to Speaking

It seems that there are more and more wars in the world now. What new wars are there? Make a presentation and briefly introduce one of the wars, including its causes, countries involved and consequences.

# Progress Against Corruption[1]

Efforts accelerate to make governments more transparent and accountable.

*By Dan Johnson*

[1] Corruption in governments throughout the world used to be considered a fact of life: undesirable, but not especially harmful. Now that attitude has changed, according to Peter Richardson, a board member of Transparency International, a corruption-fighting organization.

[2] "High levels of corruption are no longer regarded as inevitable. Consensus now exists that corrupt behavior reduces economic growth and can destabilize governments," writes Richardson in his contribution to *Managing Global Issues*, a collection of essays about global governance.

[3] Corruption erodes respect for the law and deters honest people from entering public service. It results in over-invoicing and substandard work by contractors and reduces tax revenues. Corruption also undercuts environmental regulations and building code regulations, discourages foreign direct investment in developing countries, and facilitates other crimes, such as drug trafficking, according to Richardson.

[4] Corruption scandals in the 1990s (in France, Brazil, Japan, Pakistan, and elsewhere) demonstrated that corruption is widespread, even in democracies. In recent years, government leaders and nongovernmental organizations have developed a variety of strategies to expose corruption and counter its effects.

[5] Transparency International, a global organization with 80 chapters, builds anticorruption coalitions with governments, business people, and representatives of civil society. The World Bank and the International Monetary Fund focus on introducing reforms in developing countries to address the demand side of bribery. In cases where a country has high levels of corruption and a government that is not instituting reforms, international financial institutions

---

1. Adopted from *The Futurist*, March—April, 2002

may reduce or eliminate aid. In 1996 the UN General Assembly approved a code of conduct for public officials and called on member states to make bribing public officials a crime.

[6] Corruption reform programs have had success in exposing government bribery by conducting national surveys and publishing "report cards" that detail specific instances of corruption. "Big Mac Indexes", which reveal suspicious cost differences in a country for similar commodities, such as a school lunch or a bottle of aspirin, can be especially effective, according to Richardson.

[7] "Transparency International/Argentina conducted a Big Mac survey, which revealed that a school lunch in Buenos Aires cost the equivalent of $5. A comparable lunch in Mendoza, which had been implementing anticorruption measures, cost the equivalent of 80¢. Within days of publication of the survey's results, the cost of a school lunch in Buenos Aires was more than halved," Richardson writes.

[8] Transparency International also publishes two annual reports that put pressure on governments tolerating high levels of corruption.

* The Corruption Perception Index ranks countries according to levels of corruption revealed by a composite of 14 surveys of business people, academics, and country analysts.

* The Bribe Payers Index focuses on the supply side of corruption by ranking countries according to how many bribes are offered by their international businesses.

[9] Putting a media spotlight on corruption helps to raise public awareness of the issue and can be an effective tool in combating corruption in developed countries. But attacking government corruption in the developing world will require reforms that curb the opportunities and incentives for bribery and extortion, increase the risks that corrupt behavior will be detected, and hand down severe penalties for bribery. However, many developing countries lack one or more components of the infrastructure needed to combat corruption.

[10] "The prerequisites for anticorruption reform include governmental checks and balances, a respect for the rule of law, independent judiciaries, competent prosecutorial capabilities, financial disclosure standards, free and independent media, and an expectation that bribery is not necessary in business relations," writes Richardson.

[11] One pragmatic approach to corruption reform can produce rapid results by severely prosecuting and punishing bribery in particular places. These "islands of integrity" may focus on a single city, a large building contract, or an industry segment such as power generation. For instance, all bidders on a contract are required in writing to adopt a code of conduct, provide financial reports, and submit to monitoring. Breaches of the agreement can result in legal action or international arbitration. In recent years, the "islands of integrity" approach has been applied to a refinery rehabilitation project in Ecuador, a subway construction project in Argentina, and a telecommunications privatization plan in Colombia.

[12] Although reducing worldwide corruption is no longer viewed as a quixotic undertaking, considerable obstacles remain—governments too disorganized to mount reform efforts, lax enforcement, and the resourcefulness of those who benefit from corruption. In order to be effective, reform efforts will require much time and many strategies.

[13] "Silver bullet solutions are a recipe for disaster. Building coalitions and mixing options are a slow and often frustrating way to make a difference, but for many global challenges, it is often the only effective way," write P. J. Simmons and Chantal de Jonge Oudraat of the Carnegie Endowment for International Peace.

## Useful Expressions

| | |
|---|---|
| tax revenue | 税收 |
| environment regulations | 环境调控 |
| code regulations | 法规 |
| drug trafficking | 毒品走私 |
| anticorruption organizations | 反腐败组织 |
| the demand side of bribery | 受贿方 |
| a code of conduct for public officials | 公务员行为规范 |
| a quixotic undertaking | 堂吉诃德式的事业 |

## Notes

1. Transparency International (Para.1): "透明国际",简称TI,是一个非政府、非盈利、国际性的民间组织,全球知名的反腐败机构。"透明国际"于1993年由德国人彼得·艾根创办,总部设在德国。
2. over-invoicing (Para.3) 多开发票
3. Big Mac Indexes (Para.6): 此指数试图使货币汇率理论更容易理解,它可能是世界上以快餐食品为基础的最准确的金融指数。汉堡经济学家基于购买力平价(purchasing-power parity, PPP)理论之上,认为1美元在所有的国家应该买到同样多的商品。以遍布120个国家的麦当劳的Big Mac为例,它的PPP即货币法定汇率,说明这种食品在美国和美国以外的国家价格是相同的。把实际汇率和PPP相比较可知一种货币是否被过低或过高估价了。
4. Mendoza (Para.7) 门多萨(阿根廷西部城市,门多萨省省会)
5. ¢ (Para.7): cent(s)
6. halve (Para.7): 动词指"对半分"
7. The Corruption Perception Index (Para.8): 受贿指数,由腐败研究网络中心(The Internet Center for Corruption Research)提供的对国家的廉洁行为的相对评价。
8. The Bribe Payers Index (Para.8): 行贿指数(BPI),以Gallup国际协会对15种新兴市场经济的调查为基础,显示一个国家贿赂国外政府官员的程度。
9. islands of integrity (Para.11): "廉洁岛"行动,发起于1997年7月的Caux工商大会的开幕式,目的是与全球性腐败做斗争。
10. international arbitration (Para.11) 国际仲裁
11. Silver bullet solutions are a recipe for disaster. (Para.13) 子弹是解决灾难性问题的办法。

## Exercises

### I. Reading Comprehension

*Answer the following questions according to the article.*

1. What was the public attitude toward corruption in governments?

2. What effects can corruption in governments have on society?
   _____

3. List the measures that can expose corruption and counter its effects.
   a. _____
   b. _____
   c. _____
   d. _____

4. Why is "a school lunch" mentioned in the 6th and 7th paragraph?
   _____

5. The prerequisites for the anti-corruption reform include:
   a. _____;
   b. _____;
   c. _____;
   d. _____;
   e. _____;
   f. _____;
   g. _____.

6. How can the "islands of integrity" approach reduce corruption?
   _____

7. What is the effective way to reduce corruption according to the article?
   _____

## II. Vocabulary Development

### A. Decide the meaning of the italics according to the contexts.

1. Corruption also undercuts environmental regulations and building code regulations, discourages foreign direct investment in developing countries, and facilitates other crimes, such as drug *trafficking*, according to Richardson.
   A. transportation    B. trade    C. conveyance    D. movements

2. But attacking government corruption in the developing world will require reforms that curb the opportunities and incentives for bribery and extortion, increase the risks that corrupt behavior will be detected, and *hand down* severe penalties for bribery.
   A. pass on    B. inherit    C. issue    D. spread

3. Although reducing worldwide corruption is no longer viewed as a quixotic undertaking, considerable obstacles remain—governments too disorganized to *mount* reform efforts, lax enforcement, and the resourcefulness of those who benefit from corruption.

    A. climb          B. intensify      C. install        D. jump onto
4. Although reducing worldwide corruption is no longer viewed as a quixotic undertaking, considerable obstacles remain—governments too disorganized to mount reform efforts, lax enforcement, and the *resourcefulness* of those who benefit from corruption. In order to be effective, reform efforts will require much time and many strategies.
    A. cleverness at finding ways of doing things    B. plenty of resources
    C. imaginations                                  D. raw materials

**B. Fill in the blanks with proper words.**

1. Parents are regarded _____ being responsible for the control of their children.
2. The huge waves deterred him _____ going swimming.
3. What success did you have _____ finding a new job?
4. The brutality resulted _____ as many as 300 fatalities.
5. The criminal shows a lack of respect _____ the law.

## III. From Reading to Speaking

   **Pair work:** The campaign against corruption and for clean government is the most important among all the top priorities in China. Work with your partner and make a list of phrases that are used to describe this campaign, and then translate these phrases into English.

# Part C Unit Assignments

1. People now are arguing about the possibility of globalization, and we seem to be more and more affected by other countries. Write an essay to state your point of view. Do you think globalization possible? What can be globalized: culture, finance or politics? What problems will we have in a globalized world? Support your opinion with specific examples.
2. List the questions you still have after reading these three articles.
3. List at least 10 expressions and sentence structures with meanings you have found in these three articles, and try to make your own sentences with them.

# Unit 8
# Economics

# Part A
# Lead-in

## Tax Havens Have No Economic Justification, Say Top Economists[1]

Thomas Piketty and Jeffrey Sachs among signatories of letter urging world leaders at UK anti-corruption summit to lift secrecy.

*By Patrick Wintour*

[1] More than 300 economists, including Thomas Piketty, are urging world leaders at a London summit this week to recognise that there is no economic benefit to tax havens, demanding that the veil of secrecy that surrounds them be lifted.

[2] David Cameron agreed to host the summit nearly a year ago, but the event is in danger of simply turning a spotlight on how the British government has failed to persuade its overseas territories to stop harbouring secretly stored cash.

[3] British officials are locked in negotiations with the crown dependencies and overseas territories, trying to persuade them to agree to a form of automatic exchange of information on beneficial ownership of companies. So far the overseas territories

---

1. Adopted from *The Guardian*, May 9, 2016

have only agreed to allow UK law enforcement agencies access to a privately held register of beneficial ownership, but the automatic exchange agreement would give a wider range of countries access to information on the ownership of shell companies.

[4] Many overseas territories including the Cayman Islands are resisting the idea, and their attendance at the summit is in doubt.

[5] Apart from Piketty, author of the bestselling Capital in the Twenty-First Century, the impressive roll call of economists includes Angus Deaton, the Edinburgh-born 2015 Nobel prize-winner for economics, and Ha-Joon Chang, the highly regarded development economist at Cambridge University.

[6] Other signatories include Nora Lustig, professor of Latin American economics at Tulane University, as well as influential experts who advise policymakers, such as Jeffrey Sachs, director of Columbia University's Earth Institute and an adviser to UN secretary general Ban Ki-moon, and Olivier Blanchard, former IMF chief economist.

[7] In total 47 academics from British universities, including Oxford and the London School of Economics, have signed the letter which argues that tax evasion weakens both developed and developing economies, as well as driving inequality.

[8] The signatories state: "Territories allowing assets to be hidden in shell companies or which encourage profits to be booked by companies that do no business there are distorting the working of the global economy."

[9] To counter this, they are urging governments to agree new global rules requiring companies to publicly report taxable activities in every country in which they operate, and ensure all territories publicly disclose information about the real owners of companies and trusts. A concerted drive by the EU is now under way to require companies to declare where their profits are made, and to ensure tax is paid there rather than in the country in which it is declared.

[10] In a tough broadside against the British prime minister, Jeffrey Sachs said: "Tax havens do not just happen. The British Virgin Islands did not become a tax and secrecy haven through its own efforts. These havens are the deliberate choice of major governments, especially the United Kingdom and the United States, in partnership with major financial, accounting, and legal institutions that move the money.

[11] "The abuses are not only shocking, but staring us directly in the face. We didn't need the Panama Papers to know that global tax corruption through the havens is rampant, but we can say that this abusive global system needs to be brought to a rapid end. That is what is meant by good governance under the global commitment to sustainable development."

[12] More than half of the companies set up by Mossack Fonseca, the law firm at the centre of the Panama Papers leak, were incorporated in British overseas territories such as the British Virgin Islands.

[13] The signatories admit: "Taking on the tax havens will not be easy; there are powerful vested interests that benefit from the status quo. But it was Adam Smith who said that the rich 'should contribute to the public expense, not only in proportion to their revenue, but something more than in that proportion'. There is no economic justification for allowing the continuation of tax havens which turn that statement on its head."

[14] Oxfam, which coordinated the letter, is urging the UK government to intervene to ensure that Britain's offshore territories follow its lead by introducing full public registers showing who controls and profits from companies incorporated there.

[15] Oxfam estimates that Africa loses about $14bn (£10bn) in tax revenues annually—enough money to pay for healthcare that could save 4 million children's lives a year and employ enough teachers to get every African child into school.

[16] Mark Goldring, chief executive of Oxfam GB, said, "It's not good enough for information about company owners in UK-linked tax havens to be available only to HMRC—it needs to be fully public to ensure that governments and people around the world can claim the money they are owed and hold tax dodgers to account."

Unit 8　Economics

 **Answer the following questions.**

1. What did the top economists in the world urge the world leaders to do?

2. Who are the top economists?

3. Why did the economists urge the world leaders?

4. What are tax heavens?

5. When and where did the economists do so?

# Part B
# Reading

# The Problem with Profits[1]

| Big firms in the United States have never had it so good. Time for more competition. |

*Editorial*

### Pre-reading Questions

1. What are the problems of profits?
2. Can a company make profits for ever? If not, why?
3. How can you make more profits if you have a company?
4. What kind of businesses can be profitable in recent years?

*Your questions before reading the article:*

1. _____
2. _____
3. _____
4. _____
5. _____

---

1. Adopted from *The Economist*, Mar. 26, 2016

*Words you know related to this topic:*

__profit__ _____ _____ _____
_____ _____ _____ _____
_____ _____ _____ _____

[1] America used to be the land of opportunity and optimism. Now opportunity is seen as the preserve of the elite: two-thirds of Americans believe the economy is rigged in favour of vested interests. And optimism has turned to anger. Voters' fury fuels the insurgencies of Donald Trump and Bernie Sanders and weakens insiders like Hillary Clinton.

[2] The campaigns have found plenty of things to blame, from free-trade deals to the recklessness of Wall Street. But one problem with American capitalism has been overlooked: a corrosive lack of competition. The naughty secret of American firms is that life at home is much easier: their returns on equity are 40% higher in the United States than they are abroad. Aggregate domestic profits are at near-record levels relative to GDP. America is meant to be a temple of free enterprise. It isn't.

## Borne by the USA

[3] High profits might be a sign of brilliant innovations or wise long-term investments, were it not for the fact that they are also suspiciously persistent. A very profitable American firm has an 80% chance of being that way ten years later. In the 1990s the odds were only about 50%. Some companies are capable of sustained excellence, but most would expect to see

1. Why?

2. Then what have happened with the anger?

3. What to blame?
4. Why is the problem overlooked?
5. What secret?
6. What shows that life at home is easier?

7. It isn't _____. Why?

8. What was borne by the USA?

9. Who can persistently get profits?
10. What chance can a profitable firm have?

their profits competed away. Today, incumbents find it easier to make hay for longer.

[4] You might think that voters would be happy that their employers are thriving. But if they are not reinvested, or spent by shareholders, high profits can dampen demand. The excess cash generated domestically by American firms beyond their investment budgets is running at $800 billion a year, or 4% of GDP. The tax system encourages them to park foreign profits abroad. Abnormally high profits can worsen inequality if they are the result of persistently high prices or depressed wages. Were America's firms to cut prices so that their profits were at historically normal levels, consumers' bills might be 2% lower. If steep earnings are not luring in new entrants, that may mean that firms are abusing monopoly positions, or using lobbying to stifle competition. The game may indeed be rigged.

[5] One response to the age of hyper-profitability would be simply to wait. Creative destruction takes time: previous episodes of peak profits—for example, in the late 1960s—ended abruptly. Silicon Valley's evangelicals believe that a new era of big data, blockchains and robots, is about to munch away the fat margins of corporate America. In the past six months the earnings of listed firms have dipped a little, as cheap oil has hit energy firms and a strong dollar has hurt multinationals.

[6] Unfortunately the signs are that incumbent firms are becoming more entrenched, not less. Microsoft is making double the profits it did when

11. How can it be?

12. What are they?
13. Are high profits reinvested?

14. Why was the subjunctive mood used here?

15. What game may be controlled in a dishonest way?
16. Then what can be done to solve this problem?
17. How long will it take?

18. What made the profits dropped?

19. Can this solve the problem?
20. What signs show the more strengthened profits?

antitrust regulators targeted the software firm in 2000. Our analysis of census data suggests that two-thirds of the economy's 900-odd industries have become more concentrated since 1997. A tenth of the economy is at the mercy of a handful of firms—from dog food and batteries to airlines, telecoms and credit cards. A $10 trillion wave of mergers since 2008 has raised levels of concentration further. American firms involved in such deals have promised to cut costs by $150 billion or more, which would add a tenth to overall profits. Few plan to pass the gains on to consumers.

[7] Getting bigger is not the only way to squish competitors. As the mesh of regulation has got denser since the 2007–2008 financial crisis, the task of navigating bureaucratic waters has become more central to firms' success. Lobbying spending has risen by a third in the past decade, to $3 billion. A mastery of patent rules has become essential in health care and technology, America's two most profitable industries. And new regulations do not just fence big banks in: they keep rivals out.

[8] Having limited working capital and fewer resources, small companies struggle with all the forms, lobbying and red tape. This is one reason why the rate of small-company creation in America has been running at its lowest levels since the 1970s. The ability of large firms to enter new markets and take on lazy incumbents has been muted by an orthodoxy among institutional investors that companies should focus on one activity and keep margins high. Warren Buffett, an investor, says he likes companies with "moats" that

21. Any other ways?

22. How to navigate the bureaucratic waters?

23. What are the new regulations?
24. How to keep rivals out?

25. What is the reason?

26. What wakened the ability of large firms to become bigger and stronger?

protect them from competition. America Inc has dug a giant defensive ditch around itself.

[9] Most of the remedies dangled by politicians to solve America's economic woes would make things worse. Higher taxes would deter investment. Jumps in minimum wages would discourage hiring. Protectionism would give yet more shelter to dominant firms. Better to unleash a wave of competition.

[10] The first step is to take aim at cosseted incumbents. Modernising the antitrust apparatus would help. Mergers that lead to high market share and too much pricing power still need to be policed. But firms can extract rents in many ways. Copyright and patent laws should be loosened to prevent incumbents milking old discoveries. Big tech platforms such as Google and Facebook need to be watched closely: they might not be rent-extracting monopolies yet, but investors value them as if they will be one day. The role of giant fund managers with crossholdings in rival firms needs careful examination, too.

## Set them free

[11] The second step is to make life easier for startups and small firms. Concerns about the expansion of red tape and of the regulatory state must be recognised as a problem, not dismissed as the mad rambling of anti-government Tea Partiers. The burden placed on small firms by laws like Obamacare has been material. The rules shackling banks have led them to cut back on serving less profitable smaller customers. The pernicious spread of occupational licensing has

27. What kind of companies do American investors like?
28. What are the remedies dangled by politicians?
29. How do these remedies make things worse?
30. Then what should be done to solve the problem?
31. How to unleash competition?
32. Who are spoilt incumbents?

33. How can life become easier for startups and small firms?
34. What is the existing situation of the small firms?
35. What does the word "them" refer to?

stifled startups. Some 29% of professions, including hairstylists and most medical workers, require permits, up from 5% in the 1950s.

[12] A blast of competition would mean more disruption for some: firms in the S&P 500 employ about one in ten Americans. But it would create new jobs, encourage more investment and help lower prices. Above all, it would bring about a fairer kind of capitalism. That would lift Americans' spirits as well as their economy.

36. What can improve both Americans' spirits and economy?

 **Useful Expressions**

| | |
|---|---|
| vested interests | 既得利益 |
| make hay | 把握时机 |
| depressed wages | 低薪 |
| creative destruction | 创造性破坏 |
| corporate America | 美国企业 |
| working capital | 营运资本 |
| red tape | 官僚气息 |
| economic woes | 经济困境 |
| antitrust apparatus | 反垄断机制 |
| listed firms | 上市公司 |
| institutional investors | 金融机构投资者，有组织的集体投资者 |
| rent-extracting monopolies | 抽租垄断企业 |

**Notes**

1. The campaigns have found plenty of things to blame, from free-trade deals to the recklessness of Wall Street. (Para.2) 总统团队（把此）归咎于很多东西，从自由贸易协议到华尔街的鲁莽轻率。

   这里 campaign 指上文提到的总统竞选投票情况，from free-trade deals to the recklessness of Wall Street 是 things to blame 的同位语，用于解释说明。

2. ... their returns on equity are 40% higher in the United States than they are abroad. (Para.2) ……它们在美国获得的盈利要比他们在国外获得的盈利高 40%。

   they 指代 their returns。

3. High profits might be a sign of brilliant innovations or wise long-term investments, were it not for the fact that they are also suspiciously persistent. (Para.3) 要不是令人可疑地持续，高利润可能是成功的改革或智慧的长期投资的标志。

   were it not for... 是虚拟条件句的倒装语序，正常语序为：if it were not for...。

4. Were America's firms to cut prices so that their profits were at historically normal levels, consumers' bills might be 2% lower. (Para.4) 如果美国公司准备降低价格来保证他们的利润处于历史正常水平的话，顾客们的账单便可以降低 2% 了。

   本句为虚拟条件从句的倒装语序，正常语序为：If America's firms were to cut...，从句中又包含了一个 so that 引导的目的状语从句。

5. If steep earnings are not luring in new entrants, that may mean that firms are abusing monopoly positions, or using lobbying to stifle competition. (Para.4) 如果过高的收入不准备吸引新成员的话，那就意味着公司在滥用垄断地位，或者在通过政府游说阻止竞争。

   本句需注意 abuse 的含义。

6. blockchains (Para.5)：数据区块链，比特币金融系统中的重要概念，记录了整个比特币网络上的交易记录数据，并且这些数据是被所有比特币节点共享的，通过数据区块，我们可以查询到每一笔比特币交易的历史。

7. Unfortunately the signs are that incumbent firms are becoming more entrenched, not less. (Para.6)（然而）不幸的是，迹象是现任公司（的利润）并没有变少，而是越来越稳固了。

8. As the mesh of regulation has got denser since the 2007-08 financial crisis, the task of navigating bureaucratic waters has become more central to firms' success. (Para.7) 由于自2007年至2008年经济危机以来政府规定越来越严格，应付政府的各种繁文缛节就成了公司成功的关键。

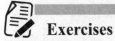

## Exercises

### I. Reading Comprehension

*Finish the following tasks.*

1. What are the problems of profits in the USA?
   _____

2. What are the causes of the problem?
   _____

3. What should be done to solve the problems?
   a. _____
   b. _____

4. (T/F) In order to make persistent high profits, American firms mostly invest their profits again or lower down their product prices.

5. (T/F) The religious people in Silicon Valley believe that big data, blockchains and robots is to take away the profits of corporate America.

6. From Paragraphs 5 and 6, we can learn about American economy that _____.
   A. history will repeat itself if we are patient enough
   B. the hyper-profitability today is not like the peak profits in 1960s
   C. a new era of big data, credit cards, batteries, airlines and blockchains is coming
   D. creative construction will make those highly-profitable companies end in the near future

7. Since the 2007-08 financial crisis, the main task of an American firm is to _____.

8. To squish competitors, the big firms _____.

### II. Vocabulary Development

**A. Please answer the questions according to the contexts.**

1. Voters' fury *fuels* the insurgencies of Donald Trump and Bernie Sanders and *weakens* insiders like Hillary Clinton.

→ Who may get more votes of the presidential election?

2. The *naughty* secret of American firms is that life at home is much easier.
   → What kind of secret is it?

3. High profits might be a sign of brilliant innovations or wise long-term investments, were it not for the fact that *they* are also suspiciously persistent.
   → What are "they"?

4. The tax system encourages them to *park* foreign profits abroad.
   → What do they do with their profits?

5. What do the italic words mean in the sentences?
   → If steep earnings are not luring in new entrants, that may mean that firms are *abusing* monopoly positions, or using lobbying to stifle competition.
   → companies should focus on one activity and keep *margins* high.
   → Copyright and patent laws should be loosened to prevent incumbents *milking* old discoveries.
   → The burden placed on small firms by laws like Obamacare has been *material*.

**B. Fill in the blanks with proper words.**

1. Now our main task is to take aim _____ the problem and try to get it solved.
2. I've noticed you have been munching _____ on lots of fruit and vegetables recently.
3. Investors also need to ensure structured notes are not _____ the mercy of volatile, or falling, equity markets.
4. Here they found a handful _____ guardsmen, and an officer, who, seeing that they were strangers, questioned their presence in the palace.
5. They closed the door and all the windows to keep the smoke _____.

## III. From Reading to Speaking

Students can be asked to find information by themselves and prepare to make a presentation in class including the following information:

1. What are the tax systems in the USA and China?

2. What are the differences of these two systems?

3. Which system do you prefer and why?

# Reading Strategy

## 如何应付生词

每位读者在阅读过程中都有可能遇到生词，而通常情况下又没有足够的时间查字典。那么读者应该学会猜测词义。要比较准确地猜测词义，读者需要学会寻找线索和提示，在平时练习时可按照以下步骤进行：

第一步：确定词性。

第二步：确定该词在所在句中的功能，也就是，它和其他词是什么关系？

第三步：寻找与之关联的上下文线索，包括同义词、反义词、指代词、句际关系（关联词、提示词等）、举例、语域，以及标点符号等。

第四步：确定词义。

这四步看起来比较烦琐，但凡事熟能生巧。请看下例。

**例** The pro-hanging lobby uses four main arguments to support its call for the reintroduction of capital punishment. First there is the deterrence theory (What is deterrence theory? →), which argues that potential murders would think twice before committing the act if they knew that they might die if they were caught. The armed bank robber might, likewise, go back to being unarmed.

In this paragraph, "deterrence" means _____.

A. proclamation      B. protest      C. prevention      D. protection

**解析** 第一步：根据词形和所在位置可以肯定它是名词。

第二步：它是后面的 theory 的定语，即名词做定语。

第三步：which 引导的非限制性定语从句用于对 deterrence theory 进行解释，本句的意思是：这种理论认为如果他们知道一旦被抓住就会判死刑的话，他们在进行谋杀活动前就会多考虑考虑。

第四步：由非限制性定语从句可知 deterrence 的意义为 C. prevention（预防，防止）。proclamation（声明）、protest（抗议）和 protection（保护）都不合从句的意思。

**练习** 请根据上下文，按照上面的方法，试着猜出下列斜体字的意义。

1. Reich tells how his own life changed the day he first realized that he had become so absorbed in his duties as US secretary of labor that he had little time or interest left for any other part of life—even his family. Reich's personal solution was to *resign* his Cabinet post and return to the calmer lifestyle of a university professor.

2. There's nothing more frustrating than sitting in a restaurant near someone who is *blaring* personal business on the phone but just a wee bit too quietly for you to hear. This can be remedied by tiny speakers on each table that can be tuned—like a radio—to any surrounding table.

# Evaluating Good Corporate Citizenship[1]

Being a good company increasingly means more than just making a profit.

By Cynthia G. Wagner

[1] Social responsibility is no longer the enemy of good business: Increasing numbers of mutual funds are adding "social screens" to their investment criteria, such as whether the fund invests in businesses that are committed to workforce diversity or to improving the environment. Though most business journals continue to trumpet the most profitable corporations, *Business Ethics* spotlights the best corporate citizens.

[2] The top honor for 2001 goes to Procter and Gamble, which moved up from number four in 2000, *Business Ethics* reports in its March-April 2001 issue. The giant consumer products company scored high in the category of "service to international stakeholders", a measure of how well the company behaves in the 44 countries outside of the United States in which it does business. P&G "has been generous in international grants and gifts in these communities, including earthquake relief in Turkey, community building projects in Japan, plus contributions for schools in China, school computers in Romania, special education in Malaysia, and shore protection in France", according to the magazine.

1. Why?
2. What are social screens?

3. Who is the best company according to *Business Ethics*?

4. Why does Procter and Gamble get the top honor?

5. How well does Procter and Gamble behave?
6. How generous?

---

1. Adopted from *The Futurist*, Jul. 2001

[3] Following P&G in the top 10 are Hewlett-Packard, Fannie Mae, Motorola, IBM, Sun Microsystems, Herman Miller, Polaroid, The St. Paul Companies, and Freddie Mac.

[4] "The term 'corporate citizenship' is coming into broader use these days, as awareness grows that business has responsibilities beyond profits," write *Business Ethics* editor Marjorie Kelly and management professors Sandra Waddock and Samuel Graves. "There is no single indicator of good citizenship. It must be measured through lenses representing various viewpoints."

[5] The magazine has been ranking corporate citizenship for five years, at first using data collected in-house, then in 2000 adding data from Kinder, Lydenberg, Domini & Co. (KLD), a social-research firm in Boston whose data serves as the basis for the Domini 400 Social Index. For 2001, *Business Ethics* further refined its rating system, adding the environment, minorities, and non-US stakeholders to the previous list of stakeholders: stockowners, customers, employees, and the community.

[6] "In addition to stockholders, other stakeholders also make investments in companies," the authors note. "Employees invest their time and their intellectual capital. Customers invest their... trust and repeated business. Communities provide infrastructure and education of future employees, in addition to more direct investments of tax supports. And so on."

[7] All of the companies of the Standard & Poor 500, plus 150 other publicly owned companies, are

7. Why is the term being used widely?

8. How can "corporate citizenship" be evaluated?

9. What kinds of viewpoints?

10. How does the magazine rank the citizenship?

11. How was the rating system refined?

12. Who are stakeholders?

13. What are the stakeholders' investments?

ranked on a standardized scale measuring the various stakeholder ratings. And to further ensure that only good corporate citizens make it onto the list, the magazine did a scandal scan: "We did a search of the Lexis database of news sources on each company to look for scandals or improprieties not detected in the KLD data. As a last check, we submitted the rankings to a board of experts for review." Among the companies dropped from the list during this process were Ben & Jerry's, which had been acquired by Unilever; Xerox, due to allegations of misstated financial information; and Microsoft, due to its antitrust conviction.

14. What is a scandal scan?
15. Is there any scandal found?

[8] "What corporate citizenship is about is progress toward better treatment of stakeholders," the authors conclude. "We publish this list not to certify companies as unblemished but to push the envelope on what it means to be a good corporate citizen, and to move corporations toward ever-better practices in stakeholder relations."

 **Useful Expressions**

| | |
|---|---|
| corporate citizenship | 公司的公民义务/责任 |
| social responsibility | 社会责任 |
| mutual funds | 互助金 |
| investment criteria | 投资准则 |
| be committed to sth./ doing sth. | 致力于某事/做某事 |
| workforce diversity | 劳动力多样化 |
| business journals | 商业周刊 |
| consumer products company | 消费品公司 |

| | |
|---|---|
| earthquake relief | 地震援救 |
| community building projects | 社区建设项目 |
| special education | 特殊教育 |

## Notes

1. Increasing numbers of mutual funds are adding "social screens" to their investment criteria, such as whether the fund invests in businesses that are committed to workforce diversity or to improving the environment. (Para.1)
本句为单句结构，such as 用于引出例子，说明解释前面的 investment criteria。such as 后面的 that 从句修饰说明前面的 businesses。to workforce diversity 和（are committed）to improving the environment 是并列成分，由 or 连接。注意这里的 or 不是和 whether 连用的。

2. data collected in-house (Para.5): (in-house: within the company, from the company itself) 从公司内部收集的数据，公司自己提供的数据

3. Kinder, Lydenberg, Domini & Co. (KLD) (Para.5): KLD Research & Analytics, Inc., 总部设在波士顿，为世界主要的投资机构提供研究、基准尺度（benchmarks）、咨询等服务。KLD 拥有全面的网上社会研究数据库和 DSI、BMSI、LCSI 等社会指数。

4. Domini 400 Social Index (Para.5): 简称 DSI，是已确立的衡量社会审查对企业、公司财政行为的作用的基准。此指数于 1990 年开始使用，是为社会投资者提供的审查股票证券的第一个基准尺度。

5. Standard & Poor 500 (Para.7): Standard & Poor's 创建于 1860 年，主要为评估公司业绩、投资等提供独立的分析数据，Standard & Poor 500 是世界通用的社会指数之一。此公司于 1966 年被 1888 年创建的 McGraw-Hill Inc. 公司兼并，成为其一个分支。

6. make it (Para.7): be successful

7. push the envelope on (Para.8): to challenge, to change

Unit 8　Economics

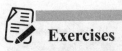 **Exercises**

## I. Reading Comprehension

*Try to answer the following questions according to the text.*

1. What is the social responsibility for a good company?

2. What did Procter and Gamble do to win the top honor for 2001?

3. How is the corporate citizenship evaluated?

4. Why are stakeholders very important to evaluate a company?

5. What is the list of good company published for?

## II. Vocabulary Development

*A. Answer the questions after each of the following sentences with the context clues.*

1. Though most business journals continue to trumpet the most profitable corporations, *Business Ethics* spotlights the best corporate citizens.
   → *Business Ethics* is _____.
   → The word "spotlight" means _____.

2. P&G has been generous in international grants and gifts in these communities, including earthquake relief in Turkey, community building projects in Japan, plus contributions for schools in China, school computers in Romania, special education in Malaysia, and shore protection in France.
   → How generous is the P&G Company?

3. For 2001, *Business Ethics* further refined its rating system, adding the environment, minorities, and non-US stakeholders to the previous list of stakeholders: stockowners, customers, employees, and the community.
   → The word "refine" means _____.
   → What is the difference of "stakeholder" and "stockholder"?

219

4. We did a search of the Lexis database of news sources on each company to look for scandals or improprieties not detected in the KLD data.
   → What do the improprieties of a company include?

**B. Fill in the blanks with proper words.**

1. I am committed _____ taking part in the meeting.
2. The term has been coming _____ broader use since 1990.
3. There is no single indicator _____ good relationship between the two countries.
4. Have you submitted your application _____ the committee for consideration?
5. The accounts were certified _____ correct.

### III. From Reading to Writing

Try to find some information about "Microsoft antitrust conviction (微软垄断案)", and write a report on it with your comments and suggestions.

# "Banker" Who Lends to the Poor Wins Nobel Peace Prize[1]

*By Philippe Naughton*

[1] The inspirational economist Muhammad Yunus was awarded the Nobel Peace Prize today for helping lift millions of his fellow Bangladeshis from poverty through a pioneering scheme that lends tiny amounts of money to the very poorest of borrowers.

[2] Professor Yunus shares the prize, and the cheque for 10 million Swedish Kronor that accompanies it, with the Grameen Bank, which he founded after the Bangladeshi famine of 1974 and whose micro-credit model has since been copied in dozens of countries around the world.

[3] The bank, which is owned almost entirely by its own borrowers, has lent out some 2.9 billion to more than 6 million Bangladeshis, 96 per cent of them women. Even though its borrowers are not asked for collateral, more than 98 percent of the money is repaid.

[4] The Norwegian Nobel Committee, which awards the Peace Prize, cited the economist and his bank for their efforts in helping to "create economic and social development from below".

[5] It added, "Lasting peace cannot be achieved unless large population groups find ways to break out of poverty. Micro-credit is one such means. Development from below also serves to advance democracy and human rights."

[6] Muhammad Yunus has shown himself to be a leader who has managed to translate visions into practical action for the benefit of millions of people, not only in Bangladesh, but in many other countries.

[7] Loans to poor people without any financial security had appeared to be an impossible idea. From modest beginnings three decades ago, Yunus has, first and foremost through Grameen

---

1. Adopted from *Times Online*, Oct. 13, 2006

Bank, developed micro-credit into an ever more important instrument in the struggle against poverty. Grameen Bank has been a source of ideas and models for the many institutions in the field of micro-credit that sprung up around the world.

[8] Every single individual on earth has both the potential and the right to live a decent life. Across cultures and civilizations, Yunus and Grameen Bank have shown that even the poorest of the poor can work to bring about their own development.

[9] Muhammad Yunus was born in Chittagong in 1940 and studied economics at Dhaka University before taking his PHD at Vanderbilt University in Tennessee, where he went as a Fulbright scholar. He returned to Bangladesh to become an economics professor at Chittagong University, where he first experimented with micro-credit after the 1974 famine.

[10] The first loan he made came from his own pocket when he lent $27 to a group of women who made bamboo furniture in a village near Chittagong. That allowed the women—who borrowed money at usurious rates to buy the bamboo—to break out of a cycle of debt and create a profitable business that could support their families.

[11] The Nobel Committee particularly praised them for having focused on female borrowers, which was also a pioneering concept.

[12] "Micro-credit has proved to be an important liberating force in societies where women in particular have to struggle against repressive social and economic conditions," it said.

[13] "Economic growth and political democracy cannot achieve their full potential unless the female, half of humanity, participates on an equal footing with the male."

[14] The citation concluded, "Yunus's long-term vision is to eliminate poverty in the world. That vision cannot be realized by means of micro-credit alone. But Muhammad Yunus and Grameen Bank have shown that, in the continuing efforts to achieve it, micro-credit must play a major part."

[15] The Nobel Peace Prize was first awarded in 1901. It was won last year by the International Atomic Energy Agency and its Egyptian head, Mohammed ElBaradei.

Unit 8　Economics

 **Useful Expressions**

| | |
|---|---|
| a pioneering scheme | 开拓型计划 |
| lift sb. from poverty | 使某人摆脱贫困 |
| the micro-credit model | 小额信贷模式 |
| cite sb. for sth. | 因某事嘉奖某人 |
| translate visions into practical action | 把理想变成实际行动 |
| live a decent life | 过一种体面的生活；过好日子 |
| at usurious rates | 按高利贷利息 |
| achieve one's full potential | 完全发挥某人的潜能 |
| on an equal footing with sb. | 与某人地位相等的基础上 |

 **Notes**

1. The inspirational economist Muhammad Yunus was awarded the Nobel Peace Prize today for helping lift millions of his fellow Bangladeshis from poverty through a pioneering scheme that lends tiny amounts of money to the very poorest of borrowers. (Para.1)
helping... 是 for 的介词宾语，意为"因帮助……"，其中 that 引导一个定语从句，修饰 a pioneering scheme，说明解释这个计划的内容。

2. Professor Yunus shares the prize, and the cheque for 10 million Swedish Kronor that accompanies it, with the Grameen Bank, which he founded after the Bangladeshi famine of 1974 and whose micro-credit model has since been copied in dozens of countries around the world. (Para.2)
it 指代 the prize，which 和 whose 引导两个非限制性定语从句，修饰 the Grameen Bank，介绍其背景材料。

3. the Bangladeshi famine of 1974

(Para.2): 孟加拉国饥荒。Possibly over a million people died in the Bangladeshi famine of 1974, from July 1974 to January 1975.

4. Micro-credit is one such means. (Para.5) = Micro-credit is one such means to help large population groups find ways to break out of poverty.

5. a Fulbright scholar (Para.9) 受美国"富布赖特项目"（The US Fulbright Scholar Program）资助赴美做研究的人员

6. "Micro-credit has proved to be an important liberating force in societies where women in particular have to struggle against repressive social and economic conditions," it said. (Para.12)
where 引导定语从句，修饰前面的 societies，即"在这个社会里，妇女尤其……"。

7. But Muhammad Yunus and Grameen Bank have shown that, in the continuing efforts to achieve it, micro-credit must play a major part. (Para.14)
it 指代上一句的 That vision，即本段第一句的 to eliminate poverty in the world

## Exercises

### I. Reading Comprehension

*Finish the following sentences according to the text.*

1. Muhammad Yunus won the Nobel _____ Prize for his _____.
2. Muhammad Yunus created _____ which has been copied by many countries.
3. Muhammad Yunus's efforts are very important in _____.
4. Yunus's ideal to creat his scheme is _____.
5. Yunus started his effort after _____.
6. The bank focuses on _____, particularly _____ because _____.

## II. Vocabulary Development

**A. Tell the meaning of the italics.**

1. ... for helping *lift* millions of his fellow Bangladeshis from poverty through a pioneering scheme that lends tiny amounts of money to the very poorest of borrowers.
2. Even though its borrowers are not asked for *collateral*, more than 98 percent of the money is repaid.
3. ... the economist and his bank for their *efforts* in helping to "create economic and social development from *below*".
4. Muhammad Yunus has shown himself to be a leader who has managed to *translate* visions into practical action for the benefit of millions of people, not only in Bangladeshi, ...

**B. Fill in the blanks with proper words.**

1. His position lifted him _____ the common world.
2. The new law has brought _____ many improvements in the employment of women.
3. How much has this bank lent _____ the company this year?
4. The school is experimenting _____ new teaching methods.
5. The boy is very brave in struggling _____ the difficulties.

## III. From Reading to Speaking

Suppose a world famous economist is invited to make a speech in our university. You are the chair-person of the speech. You are to introduce briefly the economist before the speech.

# Part C Unit Assignments

1. Write an essay with no less than 150 words discuss "Should a company make profits by hook Or by crook?" Your essay should use the information concept of this unit as examples to support your points. You can add your own data if you like.
2. List the questions you still have after reading these three articles.
3. List at least 10 expressions and sentence structures with meanings you have found in these three articles, and try to write your own sentences with them.

# Key to the Exercises

## Unit 1
## Education

### Part A   Lead-in
#### News Reading

1. They are afraid of being forced to leave Britain after last week's vote to leave EU and a potential rise in racism and community conflicts.
2. The pupils from EU who are enrolled in British schools are fearful about their future.
3. The EU referendum was the vote by British citizens to leave the European Union.
4. The British government should give pupils from EU better assurance that they will be able to complete their school education without interruption and their families remain welcome and valued members of the communities.
5. The spokesperson for the Department for Education responded that no child should live in fear of racism or bullying, and that the prime minister had been clear there would be no immediate change for EU citizens living in UK.

### Part B   Reading
#### Reading 1

**Margin Questions**
1. 参见第1段第2句。
2. 参见第1段第2句where后面的内容。
3. 参见第2段至本文结束。本问题为本文的论述重点。
4. 参见第2段第1句adoption。
5. 参见第2段第1句completion rates。
6. 参见第4~5段(无直接答案)。
7. 参见第4~5段(无直接答案)。
8. 参见第4~5段。
9. 参见第4段前两句。
10. 参见第4段五个benefits。
11. 参见第4段affordability。
12. 参见第4段Convenience。
13. 参见第4段accessibility。
14. 参见第4段accessibility中who引导的定语从句。
15. 参见第4段customizability。
16. 参见第4段preparation。
17. 参见第4段preparation中第1句。
18. 参见第4段preparation中第1句。
19. 参见第5段第1句that从句。
20. 参见第6~9段。

21. 参见第 6 段。
22. 参见第 7 段第 2 句。
23. 参见第 7 段 But 后面的内容。
24. 文中无直接答案，但从第 7 段最后一句能推断出：online education。
25. 参见第 8 段第 1 句 with 后面至段落结尾。
26. 参见第 8 段最后 1 句。

## Exercises

### I. Reading Comprehension

1. Online education.
2. Almost everyone who wants to be educated.
3. The benefits of online learning:
   a. Hundreds of lectures at elite colleges like Berkeley, Harvard, MIT and so on are available for free for participants and open to anyone.
   b. It is convenient for students to take course on their own time and at their own pace.
   c. It is accessible for people who have different backgrounds, geographies, experiences and motivations and are unlikely to attend any sort of higher education.
   d. It can be customized according to what, when, where, why, how and how much the students want to learn.
   e. It is a preparation for employees to seek jobs and increasingly a training toll in corporations.
4. there is a record high of enrollment; over 90% of the students dropped their online classes before completion
5. a. Hope to learn;
   b. Look for resources to aid other classes;
   c. Seek insights on how to teach their own class;
6. The results of online education are productive in terms of the diversity of registrants, the apparent interest of non-traditional learners, and the resultant innovation.
7. No, the online learning cannot replace the tradition classroom yet because only a small number of universities or colleges are implementing or planning to implement online course.

### II. Vocabulary Development

*A.*
1. Share.
2. → Classroom teacher.
   → Online learning systems.
3. → Low completion rates.
4. → Online learning.
   → Those who cannot attend colleges.
   → For-profit colleges.
5. → Things we can get. Results./Profits.

*B.*
1. with
2. on
3. for
4. of
5. at

## III. From Reading to Speaking

Open.

**Useful Expressions**

How to agree strongly with an opinion

I couldn't agree more!

That's absolutely true!

Absolutely!

I take your point.

I'd go along with you there.

I'm with you on that.

That's just what I was thinking.

That's a good point.

That's just how I see it.

That's exactly my opinion.

## Reading Strategy

1. Where does the call come from?
   Why is your call everybody's business?
2. What's the relationship between poverty and affluence?
   What does "success" really mean?
   How can we choose our success?
   Can being the US secretary of labor be regarded as success, and why?

## Reading 2

**Margin Questions**

1. 参见第1~2段。
2. 参见第3段第1句。
3. 参见第3段第1句that从句。
4. 参见第3段第2~3句。
5. 文中无答案。
6. 参见第4段第3句至段落结尾。
7. 参见第5段。
8. 参见第9段。
9. 参见第10段。
10. 参见第10段第3句。
11. 参见第10段第4句。
12. 参见第11段第2句至本段结尾。
13. 参见第11段第2句or后面的内容。
14. 本文无解释。
15. 参见第11段第1~3句。
16. 参见第12段第2句冒号后面的内容。
17. 参见第12段第3句至段落结尾及第13段。
18. 参见第15段第2句至段落结尾。
19. 参见第16段第3句冒号后面的内容。

## Exercises

### I. Reading Comprehension

1. Berlin's upside down education system.
2. To lead to the introduction of Berlin's upside down education.
3. F
4. prepare young people to cope with change and make them look forward to the change in the 21st century, decide which subjects they want to study and when they want to take an exam.
5. F
6. it cannot motivate students to learn
7. different backgrounds; relatively low
8. The biggest challenge is to find teachers who are able to adjust to the school's learning methods.
9. A school reform can be successful if the school will initiate the reform because

the educational ministries are hard to change.
10. doing

## II. Vocabulary Development

A.

1. → theory/reason/idea
2. → Ignore/Not to develop.
3. → To go to college.
   → 40% of the students of the year.
4. → Giant oil tanker.
   → Ministries are like giant oil tankers: it is hard to change them.

B.

1. for  2. into  3. on  4. at  5. from

## III. From Reading to Speaking

Open.

# Reading 3

## Exercises

### I. Reading Comprehension

1. meets state standards and has the flexibility to tailor its curriculum to meet the changing needs of the business community at the same time
2. the message from local employers if they have the skilled workforce that they need
3. 1) business
   2) the Coweta County School System
   3) West Central Technical College
   4) CEO
   5) directors
   6) team members
4. 1) more independence

2) more technical skills
3) more related to people across many different barriers
4) a higher level of work ethic
5. students; local economy
6. a. has high-school-age students taking classes with college curriculum, college instructors and college clinical rotations
   b. emphasizes work-based learning
7. college credits
8. work ethic

## II. Vocabulary Development

A.
1. C   2. D   3. C   4. A

B.
1. to   2. in   3. as   4. with   5. to

## III. From Reading to Speaking

Open.

**Useful Expressions**

**How to disagree politely with an opinion**

I am not sure really.
Do you think so?
Well, it depends.
I'm not so certain.
Well, I'm not so sure about that.
I'm inclined to disagree with that.
No, I don't think so really.

**How to disagree strongly with an opinion**

I disagree.
I disagree with you entirely.
I'm afraid I don't agree.
I'm afraid you are wrong there.
I wouldn't accept that for one minute.
You can't really mean that.

You can't be serious.
You must be joking.

# Unit 2
# Science and Technology

## Part A  Lead-in
**News Reading**

1. Lee Sedol won the fourth showdown of five series against Google's artificial intelligence, AlphaGo.
2. Lee Sedol is the 33-year-old South Korean champion Go player.
3. AlphaGo is the artificial intelligence program developed by the Google subsidiary, DeepMind.
4. AlphaGo was designed to approximate human intuition by studying old matches and using simulated games to hone itself independently.
5. Yes. IBM's DeepBlue famously beat the former world champion Garry Kasparov in 1997.

## Part B  Reading
**Reading 1**

**Margin Questions**

1-2. 参见第 2 段及第 5 段。
3. 参见第 3 段第 1 句冒号后面的内容。
4. 参见第 3 段第 2~3 句。
5. 参见第 4 段。
6. 参见第 7~8 段。
7. 参见第 10~12 段。
8. 参见第 14 段第 1 句。
9. 参见第 14 第 2 句及第 15 段。
10. 参见第 14~15 段。
11. 参见第 16 段第 2~3 句。

## Exercises

### I. Reading Comprehension

1. A digital ecosystem is a digital system created by digital companies to make users easy to embrace their offerings but hard to switch to other companies. A typical ecosystem includes a series of interconnected products and services, like hardware (phone, tablet, laptop, smartwatch, TV box); online stores (music, movies, TV, e-books); synchronization of your data across gadgets (calendar, bookmarks, notes, photographs); cloud storage (a free online "hard drive" for files); and payment systems (wave your watch or phone instead of swiping a credit card).
2. In order to lure the customers, big tech companies are racing to build the best, most enticing ecosystem.
3. A jungle can be a place or situation that is unpleasant because people are trying to achieve things for themselves and are not helping each other. Tech companies created the ecosystem in order to get more profits and guard against each other.
4. They can make a call, surf the Internet, watch movies, listen to music, pay by waving his/her watch, read, and take photos, and so on.

5. 1) looks; 2) price; 3) speed; 4) feature
   a. writes apps only for iPhones and iPads, and offer software for car dashboards and home-automation system to work with the smartphones.
   b. makes its wares available to other platforms like Mac, Windows and Linux users, and offer software for car dashboards and home-automation system to work with the smartphones.
   c. is available just about anything with a screen, as are many of its mobile apps.
   d. makes cluster of competitive products and linked services.
   e. makes phones, tablets and TV boxes.
6. what suite of products they like best; whether to open up their services to people who use their competitors' products.
7. They will be dismayed but happy because there is competition which will bring about innovation and often lower prices.

**II. Vocabulary Development**

A.
1. → A big package of/a series of interconnected products and services.
2. → Because it feels comfortable but takes away your freedom to leave.
3. → The customers are happy because each company is trying its best to offer good products and services.
4. → It is not open to the products of other companies.
5. → Microsoft Office

B.
1. into  2. in  3. to  4. in  5. on

**II. From Reading to Speaking**

Open.

**Reading Strategy**

（1）（就第1句提问）Which two ways?（参见第2句和第4句）
（2）（就第2句提问）What kind of humanitarian effort?（参见 treating 后面的内容和第3句）
（3）（就第4句提问）How much is the compensation?（参见最后一句）

**Reading 2**

**Margin Questions**

1. 参见文章主题的引子，引出让谁来干家务，以此来引出机器人。
2. 参见第2段第1句破折号后面的内容。
3. 参见第4段第一个逗号后面的内容。
4. 参见第4段冒号后面的内容。
5. 文中无叙述。
6. 参见第5段第1句：the whiz who...。
7. 参见 Google's。
8. 参见第7段破折号后面至段落结尾的内容。
9. 参见第8~10段。
10. 参见第9~10段。
11. 本文无叙述。
12. 参见第13段第2句至段落结尾。
13. 参见第14~16段。
14. 参见第16段最后一句。
15. 参见第17段第2句至段落结尾。

# Key to the Exercises

## Exercises

### I. Reading Comprehension

1. We will have robots that can take care of our life.
2. The robots will come in the not-too-distant future.
3. F
4. F
5. T
6. B
7. C
8. carry out a particular task like teaching, window-washing, working along with human, serving as a security guard, clothes-folding, and head butler
9. redundant
10. the benefits to society become large enough

### II. Vocabulary Development

A.
1. → The creator of Google's Android operating system.
2. → Well-developed.
3. → Set up a robot and teach it to make something.
4. → The robots.

B.
1. off   2. with   3. with   4. out   5. with

### III. From Reading to Speaking

Open.

## Reading 3

## Exercises

### I. Reading Comprehension

1. Near-sightedness is the Asia's myopia epidemic.
2. East Asia, especially Hong Kong and Singapore City have rates of myopia in the 80%, and South Korea 96%.
3. Get some sunlight.
4. One theory suggests that sunlight triggers the release of dopamine in the retina; another speculates that blue light from the sun protects from the condition.
5. Children don't get outside enough.
6. In Asian cultures where there is heavy emphasis on education and hyper-competitiveness, forcing playtime is easier said than done.
7. Students sit at their desks and massage the pressure points around their eyes as a revolutionary-era anthem blares through the PA system.
8. It is also called the "bright light classroom" where the school's walls and ceilings are made of see-through plastic that allows in light, which is to help students get increased exposure to sunlight.

### II. Vocabulary Development

A.
1. Objects.    2. Myopia.
3. Myopia.    4. Kids.
5. Students.

233

*B.*
1. to    2. on    3. at    4. for    5. In

**III. From Reading to Writing**

Open.

# Unit 3
# Disasters

## Part A    Lead-in

### News Reading

1. Heavy rainfall and severe flooding hit the Yangtze river basin in China this week, killing more than 180 people, dozens missing and, overall, 33 million people affected.
2. India and Pakistan suffered damaging floods over the weekend, and more than 60 people died.
3. The Australian city of Adelaide had its wettest day in 75 years on Monday, with more than 50mm recorded in 24 hours in some suburbs.
4. The holidaymakers in Spain may have experienced extreme heat in the country, with many areas exceeding 40℃. Hottest of all was Cordoba, in the province of Andalusia, where a high of 44.5℃ was measured on Sunday—about 8℃ above normal. In Madrid afternoon temperatures have topped 33℃ every day since 20 June.
5. Twenty-three people were killed by a single mudslide in Guizhou, China.

## Part B    Reading

### Reading 1

**Margin Questions**

1. 参见第2~3段内容。
2. 参见第4段第1句不定式 to build homes in high-risk areas。
3. 参见第4段第2句和第3句。
4. 参见第5段内容。
5. 参见第4段第2句内容。
6. 参见第4~6段描述的相互矛盾的现象。
7. 参见第4段第2句内容。
8. 参见第6段 which 后面的内容。

9~10. 参见第7段第2句内容。

11. 参见第8段第1句 because 后面的内容。
12. 参见第8段第1句 which 引导的非限制性定语从句。
13. 参见第9段内容。

14~15. 参见第10段内容。

16. 参见第11段内容。

## Exercises

### I. Reading Comprehension

1. natural disasters
2. explain how disasters were made worse by the propensity of people to build homes in high-risk areas
3. a) gale-force wind    b) human misery
4. should discourage people from moving to dangerous areas; encourage people to build in flood and hurricane-prone areas

5. 1) stricter building codes
   2) more aggressive land use planning
   3) is hard to carry out
6. serving as the kindling for spreading infernos
7. live in high-risk areas; result in

## II. Vocabulary Development

A.
1. Its development is as twice as the state average.
2. move to dangerous areas
3. solve
4. The building regulations that home could be built with fir-retardant materials and protective features to prevent embers from getting inside, and owners could also be required to prune away brush.

B.
1. from   2. down   3. away
4. aside   5. as

## III. From Reading to Speaking
Open.

## Reading Strategy

1. The form is of asking and answering the questions, reading the summary, and trying to fill in the details for each main idea.
2. Formed from the headings.
3. It is about the main ideas in the chapter.

## Reading 2

**Margin Questions**

1. 参见第 2 段 $15 million。
2. 参见第 2 段第 2 句 to seek loans。
3. 参见第 4 段内容。
4. 参见第 2 段第 1 句。
5. 参见第 7~8 段内容。
6. 参见第 9 段第 1 句 $40 million。
7. 参见第 9 段第 2 句 which 后面的内容。
8. 参见第 11 段 after a series of scandals, including…。

## Exercises

### I. Reading Comprehension

1. B    2. F    3. C    4. F    5. D
6. take out loans to fund their response

### II. Vocabulary Development

A.
1. → With no money left in the fund, the Red Cross has to seek loans to support its staff and volunteers.
   → The Red Cross has spent almost all the money on a large number of mid size disasters or "silent" disasters.
2. Floods.
3. → Emergency legislation.
   → No, it cannot.
   → The Red Cross will.
4. 1) conjunction
   2) pronoun: to provide services to disaster victims
   3) pronoun: to take out loans to fund our response

*B.*

1. for  2. in  3. on  4. on  5. out

### III. From Reading to Speaking

Open.

## Reading 3

## Exercises

### I. Reading Comprehension

1. Their trends to live in disaster-prone regions have increased the natural disasters.
2. The trends to live in disaster-prone regions have made the water keeps collecting and rushing down, getting heavier and faster, and then we have much bigger floods.
3. (1) A natural event if it kills 10 or more people or leaves at least 100 people injured, homeless, displaced or evacuated;

   (2) A natural event if a country declares it a natural disaster;

   (3) A natural event if the event requires the country to make a call for international assistance.
4. Earthquake and tsunami.
5. 1) artificial
   2) better media reports and advances in communications
   3) agencies actively looking for natural disasters
   4) real
   5) hydro-meteorological disasters
   6) droughts
   7) tsunamis
   8) hurricanes
   9) typhoons
   10) floods
6. A combination of natural and human-caused factors, like:

   (1) Global warming is increasing the temperatures of Earth's oceans and atmosphere, leading to more intense storms of all types, including hurricanes.

   (2) Natural decadal variations in the frequency and intensity of hurricanes.

   (3) Large-scale temperature fluctuations in the tropical waters of the Eastern Pacific Ocean, known as El Niño and La Niña.

   (4) People are also tempting nature with rapid and unplanned urbanization in flood-prone regions, increasing the likelihood that their towns and villages will be affected by flash floods and coastal floods.
7. The number of deaths has decreased substantially with the help of prevention programs, but more people are being injured, displaced or left homeless.

### II. Vocabulary Development

*A.*

1. Yes, there are many different major disasters in one year.
2. → that can be passed to others
   → to become less important
3. created by people
4. Water.

B.
1. to   2. in   3. out of
4. out   5. with

## III. From Reading to Writing

Open.

# Unit 4
# Sports

## Part A   Lead-in

### News Reading

1. Li Janrou won the gold medal in the Sochi 2014 Winter Olympics.
2. Li Jianrou won the gold medal simply by staying on her feet in a crash-filled final.
3. It was a crash-filled final where every player fell down during the game except Li Jianrou.
4. She was excited and moved, and felt lucky.
5. Arianna Fontana of Italy took the silver and Park Seung-hi of South Korea earned the bronze.

## Part B   Reading

### Reading 1

**Margin Questions**

1. 参见第 2 段至文章末尾。本问题为本文论述重点。
2. 参见 Playing sports.
3. 参见第 2 段最后一句 which 从句。
4. 参见第 3 段最后一句 by 后面的内容。
5~6. 参见第 4 段第 2 句引号里的内容。
7. 参见第 4 段最后一句。
8. 参见第 4 段引号里的内容。
9. 参见第 5 段第 1 句 in 后面的内容。
10. 参见第 6 段。
11. Sporting bodies.
12. European nationals.
13. 参见第 7 段第 2 句。
14. 参见第 7 段第 3 句 in terms of 后面的内容。
15. 参见第 8 段最后一句。
16. 参见第 9 段第 1 句 by 后面的内容及第 2 句。
17. 参见第 9 段第 2 句。
18. 参见第 9 段第 2 句 but 后面的内容。
19. 参见第 9 段最后 1 句。
20. 参见第 10 段第 2 句至段落结尾。
21. 参见第 10 段第 2 句。
22. 参见第 13 段第 1 句。
23. 参见第 13 段第 2 句。
24. 参见第 14 段第 3 句。
25. 参见第 14 段第 2 句结尾：looking to expand their audience。
26. 参见第 14 段引号里的内容。
27. The NFL.

## Exercises

### I. Reading Comprehension

1. a. be unable to play in the British sporting bodies without a work permit
   b. have to pay more and miss out on rising talents
   c. suffer a degraded status

2. 1) cricket and rugby
   2) Africa, Caribbean and Pacific Group of Sates
3. F
4. F
5. they are looking to expand their audience

**II. Vocabulary Development**

A.
1. → Playing sports.
2. → The pattern./The general situation.
3. → For example.
4. → That London is the gateway to Europe.
5. → 1) The freedom of movement principle.
   → 2) Introducing quotas of English footballers.
   → 3) The Cotonou Agreement and the Kolpak Ruling.
   → 4) That future imports from EU and so on will count as foreign players.

B.
1. with   2. to   3. out   4. as   5. for

**III. From Reading to Speaking**

Open.

## Reading Strategy

1. A   2. B   3. A   4. D

## Reading 2

**Margin Questions**

1. 参见第 2~3 段。
2. 参见第 4 段。
3. What matters?（参见第 2 段 such as 后面的内容）。
4. 参见第 4 段。
5. 参见第 5 段 to 后面的内容。
6. 参见第 7 段。
7. 参见第 9~10 段。
8. 参见第 11 段第 2 句。
9. 参见第 12 段最后一句。

## Exercises

**I. Reading Comprehension**

1. The Olympic spirit is the heart of the Olympics.
2. To educate the world's youth on matters such as doping and even some not directly related to sports such as HIV prevention.
3. The goal of the Olympic movement is to contribute to building a peaceful and better world by educating youth through sport practiced in the spirit of Olympism.
4. The education is being continued right now in China and that millions of young Chinese are being introduced to the strength and power of the Olympic values such as friendship, excellence and respect.
5. Through the staging of the Olympic Games, Beijing is willing to further reinforce the exchange with international friends and accelerate the development of China and Beijing to leave a precious legacy to China and world sports.
6. No, because young people today

are attracted by many other leisure activities such as music, video games, the Internet and movies.
7. The sports and Olympics should maintain serious efforts to maintain their interest in sport and physical activities.
8. Scientists and doctors who contribute to unethical behaviors through the misuse of drugs must be stigmatized, which can be considered another form of education.
9. The IOC intends to make the Beijing Olympics a festival of harmony and peace, education and culture and above all of sporting perfection.
10. Warning athletes about the danger to their health caused by doping was a key element to the Olympic movement's education task.

**II. Vocabulary Development**

*A.*
1. Olympic sports.
2. To contribute to building a peaceful and better world by educating youth through sport practiced in the spirit of Olympism.
3. World/Group.
4. By hosting Olympic Games.

*B.*
1. to    2. to    3. on    4. to    5. for

**III. From Reading to Speaking**

Open.

## Reading 3

**Exercises**

**I. Reading Comprehension**

1. To encourage reconciliation between the two countries.
2. They try to forget the past, and enjoy the exchange of cultures, including music, video, and movies, and begin to make friends with each other.
3. Because Japanese consider Koreans as clumsy and ill-mannered countrymen, and can't understand why Koreans can't forget the past.
4. The major reason is Korea's newfound socioeconomic equality.
5. To show that sports and music can help reconciliation between the two countries.

**II. Vocabulary Development**

*A.*
1. B    2. A    3. A    4. C

*B.*
1. up    2. out    3. to
4. on    5. with    6. down

**III. From Reading to Speaking**

Open.

# Unit 5
# Global Development

## Part A    Lead-in

### News Reading

1. The number of the people killed by

malaria dropped below half a million in 2015.
2. The use of insecticide-treated bednets, indoor and outdoor spraying, timely and appropriate treatment with easily available antimalarial medicine and so on have averted millions of deaths.
3. It is a mosquito-born disease.
4. Sub-Saharan Africa is the hardest-hit area.
5. Yes. Drug resistance to insecticides has developed in recent year, which could jeopardize the malaria control.

## Part B  Reading
### Reading 1
**Margin Questions**
1. 参见第1段第3句。
2. 参见第2段第1句。
3. 参见第3段至全文结束。
4. What's the conclusion of the argument? （参见第4~6段）。
5. What's the decision? （参见第4段第2句至第6段）。
6. 参见第4段第3句至第6段。
7. 参见第6段。
8. 参见第7段第1句citing后面的内容。
9. 参见第8段第2句至本段结束。

## Exercises
### I. Reading Comprehension
1. Gene rights.
2. the usefulness of Dolly's genes
3. Because there is no existing law in this field to guide her.
4. The Judge affirmed the legitimate right of the P sequence to the NuGenEra, but the company does not have the right to Dolly's whole genome.
5. There will be a change in the existing patent law.

### II. Vocabulary Development
A.
1. that Dolly's genes make him resistant to HIV
2. sell
3. The company.
4. B

B.
1. against    2. to    3. of
4. against    5. from

### III. From Reading to Speaking
Open.

### Reading Strategy
Open.

### Reading 2
**Margin Questions**
1. 参见第1段第2句至本段结束。
2. 参见第2段第2句至本段结束。
3. 参见第3段第2句至本段结束。
4. To make money.
5. 参见第3段第3句：provide a soul to TVT。
6. 参见第3段第1句: do these things，指代第1~2段内容。
7. 参见第3段第4句至该段结束。
8. 参见第4段第2句至第8段结束。
9. 参见第4段第3句至第5段结束。

10. 参见第 5 段。
11. 参见第 5 段最后一句。
12~13. 参见第 6 段第 2 句至本段结束。
14. 参见第 7 段最后两句。
15. 参见第 7 段第 3 句至本段结束。
16. 参见第 7 段第 5~6 句。
17. Inputs—benefits from charity work; outputs—charity work.
18. 参见第 7 段之前的所有叙述：All the charity work.
19. 参见第 8 段第 3 句至本段结束。

# Exercises

## I. Reading Comprehension

1. It is about how the charity work of companies can help themselves.
2. The charity work makes employees prouder to work at the company and it helps with the recruitment.
3. First, collaboration is in with NGOs. Second, local community work is increasingly becoming global community work. And third, once a formal programme is in place, it becomes hard to stop.
4. To explain how and why companies cooperate with NGOs.
5. The young employees get one-month assignments in the developing world to work on worthy projects, which can develop managers who understand how the wider world works.
6. They are keen on it.
7. It indicates that straightforward cash donation is less important.
8. The author thinks that cash still matters.
9. Helping others provides you a soul.
10. Helping others.

## II. Vocabulary Development

A.
1. B    2. Information
3. B    4. The young employees.

B.
1. in    2. with    3. on    4. at    5. in

## III. From Reading to Speaking

Open.

# Reading 3

# Exercises

## I. Reading Comprehension

1. This article is about Kakenya Ntaiya and what she has done to change her Kenyan village.
2. Ntaiya has challenged the traditions in her Kenyan village, including the opportunity for girls to be educated, female genital mutilation and child marriage.
3. Ntaiya has made it possible for girls to continue their education and dream big.
4. Ntaiya has changed her village by opening a school for girls.
5. Many villagers are willing to have their girls educated and keep them away from early marriage and genital mutilation.
6. a. Negotiation with her father;
   b. Encouragement from her mother;
   c. Fund-raising of her village fro her

airfare to US;

d. Her own promise to return and help her village.

7. expand her school to include lower grades; provide tutoring for those who want to head to high School; open a career center

8. 1) KakenyaNtaiya
   2) primary
   3) 150
   4) Kenyan
   5) education
   6) opportunities
   7) their dreams
   8) fourth to eighth
   9) household chores
   10) being sexually assaulted on the way to school
   11) focus on their studies
   12) financially supported
   13) meals

## II. Vocabulary Development

A.

1. → Genital mutilation and child marriage.
   → Genital mutilation and child marriage.
2. → To be educated.
   → Girls should not receive education and should marry at an early age.
3. → People from her village.
4. D
5. → Girls will not be subjected to genital mutilation or early marriage.
6. She made it possible with a school for girls to see that they can change the old customs and get a new and better life.

B.

1. with  2. for  3. off  4. to  5. to

## III. From Reading to Speaking

Open.

### Useful expressions

I want to welcome you all to...

We are greatly honored to...

Ladies and gentlemen, it is my great pleasure to present to you...

It is my pleasure to introduce the keynote speaker for tonight, ...Dr./Ms. ...

I hope that you will enjoy his/her lecture and get out of it something that will be a permanent enrichment of your lives.

The distinguished speaker who will address us on "...." is.., Dr.?Ms./Mr. ...

# Unit 6
# Environment

## Part A   Lead-in

### News Reading

1. They asked to shut down the UK's largest coalmine in order to keep fossil fuels in the ground, to stop catastrophic climate change.

2. Miller Argent declined to talk to the Guardian and a spokesman told the BBC that the discussion around climate change needed to be "more balanced" and the miners were proud of the job they did, which included supporting the steel industry. The company is applying

a new mine but is rejected.
3. The coalmine is near Merthyr Tydfil in south Wales.
4. The protesters include environmental activists and local people.
5. Dressed in red boiler suits, groups of protesters crossed barbed wire fences to gain access to the mine. Some chained themselves to machinery, others lay across access roads. Dozens of protesters, joined by local people, also blockaded the entrance to the mine's headquarters.

## Part B    Reading
### Reading 1
**Margin Questions**
1. 参见第 2 段。
2. 参见第 3 段开始至文章结束，这部分内容叙述了计算机如何被回收。
3. 参见第 2 段最后一句。
4. 参见第 3 段第 2~3 句。
5. 参见第 3 段第 3 句两个破折号之间的内容。
6. 参见第 5 段至全文结束。
7. 参见第 4 段第 2 句。
8. 参见第 4 段第 4 句。
9. 同问题 7。
10. 参见第 4 段最后一句。
11. 参见第 5 段第 1 句。
12. 参见第 5 段第 2~4 句。
13. 参见第 6 段第 1 句。
14. 参见第 6 段第 2 句。
15. 参见第 7 段之后的内容。
16. 参见第 7 段第 2 句至本段结束。
17. 参见第 8 段。
18. 参见第 8 段第 2~3 句。
19. 参见第 9~11 段。
20. How to resell the machine? (参见第 9 段第 1 句破折号后面的内容)
21. What can be done about the too old parts? (参见第 10 段)
22. 参见第 11 段。
23. 参见第 12 段。
24. Why does more work need to be done? (参见第 13 段第 2 句)
25. 参见第 14 段。

## Exercises
### I. Reading Comprehension
1. F
2. it contains toxic components
3. F
4. a. reselling the machine, either whole or for its working parts;
   b. shopping those too old parts to specialists in plastics, metals and glass;
   c. making full use of metals.
5. protecting environment from pollution is everybody's business

### II. Vocabulary Development
A.
1. extract    2. more attractive
3. ends    4. pay
B.
1. at    2. up    3. with    4. up    5. to

### III. From Reading to Writing
Open.

**Reading Strategy**

The colleges and universities in the 21st century will work together with each other in a globalized world.

**Reading 2**

**Margin Questions**

1. 参见第 1 段第 1~2 句。
2. 参见第 1 段倒数第 2 句,they 前指。
3. 参见第 2 段至文章结尾。
4. 参见第 2 段后两句。
5. 参见第 3~4 段。
6. 参见第 3 段 such as 后面的内容。
7. 参见第 4 段。
8. 参见第 4 段最后一句。
9. 参见第 6 段。
10. 参见第 6 段。
11. 参见第 6 段 Yet 后面的内容。
12. 参见第 7 段第 2 句开始至 10 段。
13. 参见第 7 段第 2 句破折号后面的内容。
14. 文中无具体论述。
15. 参见第 9 段 For example 后面的内容。
16. 参见第 10 段最后一句。
17. 参见第 7 段第 2 句。
18. 参见第 11 段最后一句。

# Exercises

## I. Reading Comprehension

1. This article mainly talks about the possible effects of climate change and its solution.
2. In recent years, we have experienced various effects of warming like more frequent hurricanes, long-term changes in rainfall and temperatures, and rising sea-levels.
3. Climate change will cause terror and conflict as well.
4. In fragile contexts, where poverty, weak governance and conflict are frequent and the ability to cope with these risks is low, climate change will increase the risk of violent conflict and is the ultimate multiplier of threats.
5. To solve the problem, (1) we need to address the lack of livelihood diversification, political marginalization, unsustainable management of natural resources, weak or inflexible institutions and unfair policy processes; (2) people and governments need to adapt; (3) better policies are required, and (4) "climate-proof" jobs are needed.
6. The main cause is the existing social, political and economic tensions.
7. This is to explain how improper policy can exacerbate riots.

## II. Vocabulary Development

A.

1. → To curb greenhouse gas emissions and to tackle the pervasive threat of terror.
2. Problem.
3. → At work.
4. → New money.
5. → Climate change adaptation, development and humanitarian aid, and peace-building.

B.

1. with   2. with   3. out   4. on   5. in

### III. From Reading to Speaking

Open.

## Reading 3

### Exercises

#### I. Reading Comprehension

1. Nobel Peace Prize winner Wangari Maathai and her Green Belt Movement
2. committed to the environment, democracy and human rights
3. planting trees; Nobel Peace Prize
4. malnutrition; lack of water; firewood; cash crops
5. African women; gave them a sense of accomplishment and self worth
6. Kenya (Africa); many other countries; women; children
7. a) discrimination at the university
   b) being treated as a second-class citizen by her husband
8. sustainable development; food security; soil and forest protection; cultural conservation
9. Green Belt Movement

#### II. Vocabulary Development

A.

1. C   2. A
3. to keep going (to start fighting back)
4. give up

B.

1. up   2. on   3. to   4. as   5. in

### III. From Reading to Speaking

Open.

# Unit 7
# Politics

## Part A   Lead-in

### News Reading

1. UK must maintain maximum involvement in EU anti-terrorism, intelligence and security policies.
2. The chairman said this after recent events in Germany, France and Belgium.
3. His major concern is that the UK had to opt in to a revised deal on how Europol is run if it is to retain its involvement and keep key UK staff at its headquarters in The Hague, beyond May next year.
4. The UK will be safer to have EU's cooperation in tracking down terrorists and international criminals.
5. A special new arrangement must be forged to keep UK remained in the EU security policies.

## Part B   Reading

### Reading 1

**Margin Questions**

1. 参见第 2 段至本文结束。
2. 参见第 3 段。

3. 参见第 3 段第 2 句结尾：undermining the idea of cooperation。
4. 参见第 3 段最后一句破折号前面的中心词 the new connectedness。
5. 参见第 5 段。
6. What problems?（参见第 5 段第 2 句破折号后面的内容）
7. What voices?（参见第 6 段第 2 句破折号后面的内容）
8. 参见第 7 段。
9. 参见第 6 段最后一句和第 7 段第 1 句 with 后面的内容。
10. Why are strong governments essential to global cooperation?（参见第 8 段第 2 句 because 至本段结束）
11. 参见第 9 段第 2 句。
12. 参见最后一段引号里内容。

## Exercises

### I. Reading Comprehension

1. economic opportunity and many problems
2. the superpowers want to impose their one-sided ideas on others
3. All societies have an equal voice.
4. a. a homogenizing effect on the world's culture;
   b. opponents of big government.
5. Strong governments are essential to global cooperation because they can contain the inequities of the market.
6. global cooperation could get a stimulus from new governing alliances within a stronger civil society beyond the state-to-state model of the past

### II. Vocabulary Development

A.
1. C
2. The new connectedness.
3. → A
   → Opportunities for both sides.
4. It can damage the hope for meaningful cooperation.

B.
1. on  2. at  3. on  4. than  5. than

### III. From Reading to Speaking

Open.

## Reading Strategy

1）首先通过三组同义词理解本段落叙述的是同一个问题：海岸线上升作为全球变暖的一个后果会立刻威胁海边大面积地区。

threaten → be endangered, be inundated, suffer extreme dislocation

large fraction of the globe → most of the world's great cities, some countries, heavily populated areas living at sea level → sea-port, islands in the Ocean/Pacific, coastal

2）利用同一句子结构表示并列的句际关系：主语 + would + 动词原形。

3）利用不同手段表示列举：标点符号（: 和 -) 和连接代词 (such as)。

## Reading 2

### Margin Questions

1. A war president.（参见第 2 段第 1 句）
2. A boomer politician.（参见第 2 段第

1 句)

3. 参见第 1 段第 4 句冒号后面的内容。
4. To test the American in the prosperous time. 参见第 1 段最后 3 句。
5. What crisis?（参见第 2 段第 1 句 and 后面的内容）
6. 参见第 2 段第 1 句 who 引导的定语从句。
7. 参见第 2 段第 1 句冒号后面的内容。
8. 参见第 2 段最后一句。
9. Why is it complicated?（参见第 3 段第 2 句至本段结束）
10. 参见第 3 段第 3 句破折号后面的内容。
11. 参见第 3 段第 4 句 one 引导的同位语。
12. 参见第 4 段第 3~5 句。
13. 参见第 5 段第 1 句破折号后面的内容。
14. The attack on September 11.
15. The war against Afghanistan Bush is fighting now.
16. 参见第 7~8 段。
17. What are these three themes?（参见第 9 段第 2 句至段尾，注意本段写作特点：利用平行句子结构表示列举 He will... He will... And he will...）

# Exercises

## I. Reading Comprehension

1. A politician facing the promise of prosperity and dealing with a budget surplus.
2. A war president with a task to fight and define a war without any precedent.
3. American wars have usually been about defeating specific enemies, toppling particular capitals, and then moving on.
4. A special kind of conflict without a definite deadline, or a long twilight struggle.
5. Bush must find a word that evokes urgency while calling for open-ended patience.
6. Objective.

## II. Vocabulary Development

A.

1. Storming beaches, liberating concentration camps and delivering us from evil (i. e. victory in World War II).
2. To use a word that evokes urgency while calling for open-ended patience.
3. Poverty, crime and drugs.
4. → Because it is more familiar to Americans.
   → the fact that the word "war" is less powerful than before
5. author/drafter

B.

1. to   2. on   3. on   4. into   5. to

## III. From Reading to Speaking

Open.

# Reading 3

# Exercises

## I. Reading Comprehension

1. The public used to take corruption for granted as an inevitable fact of life.
2. It can reduce economic growth, destabilize governments, erodes respect

for the law, and deters honest people from entering public service.

3. a. Coalitions from global organizations, governments, business and the public are built for anti-corruption.
   b. The reforms from the World Bank and the International Monetary Fund are conducted to control and punish the demand side of bribery.
   c. A code of conduct was approved by UN General Assembly for public officials in 1996.
   d. Laws were called on to make bribing public officials a crime.

4. To explain how Big Mac Index is effective to expose bribery.

5. a. governmental checks and balances
   b. a respect for the rule of law
   c. independent judiciaries
   d. competent prosecutorial capabilities
   e. financial disclosure standards
   f. free and independent media
   g. an expectation that bribery is not necessary in business relations

6. Through a code of conduct and open financial report for monitoring.

7. Building coalitions and mixing options.

## II. Vocabulary Development

A.
1. B   2. C   3. B   4. A

B.
1. as   2. from   3. in
4. in   5. for

## III. From Reading to Speaking

Open.

# Unit 8
# Economics

## Part A   Lead-in

### News Reading

1. The top economists urged the world leaders to lift the secrecy of the tax heavens and agree new rules requiring companies to public report taxable activities in every country in which they operate, and ensure all territories publicly disclose information about the real owners of companies and trusts.

2. There are more than 300 economists, including Thomas Piketty, the author of the bestselling Capital in the Twenty-First Century, Angus Deaton, the Edinburgh-born 2015 Nobel prize-winner for economics, and Ha-Joon Chang, the highly regarded development economist at Cambridge University, Jeffrey Sachs, director of Columbia University's Earth Institute and an adviser to UN secretary general Ban Ki-moon, and so on.

3. They think that tax havens have no justification and tax evasion weakens both developed and developing economies, as well as driving inequality. For example, Africa loses about $14bn in tax revenues annually—enough money to pay for healthcare that could save 4 million children's lives and employ enough teachers to get every African child into school.

4. Tax heavens are overseas places for companies to evade taxes. It refers to those overseas territories of Britain, the US, etc. which allow assets to be hidden in shell companies or which encourage profits to be booked by companies that do no business there. The Cayman Islands and the British Virgin Islands are two typical examples.

5. The economists urged the governments at the UK anti-corruption summit in 2016.

## Part B Reading

### Reading 1

**Margin Questions**

1. 参见第 1 段第 2 句冒号后面的内容。
2. 参见第 1 段最后一句。
3. 参见第 2 段第 1 句逗号后面的内容。
4. 参见第 2 段第 2 句冒号后面的内容。
5. 参见第 2 段第 3 句 that 后面的内容。
6. 参见第 2 段第 3 句冒号后面的内容。
7. It isn't a temple of free enterprise.
本句是文章的论点句，第三段开始解释。
8. The economic situation.
9. 参见第 3 段最后一句。
10. 参见第 3 段第 1 句，that way 前指。
11. 参见第 4 段。
12. 参见第 4 段第二句：high profits。
13. 参见第 4 段第 3 句及其之后的内容。
14. 参见第 4 段最后一句。
15. 本文的主题词：To keep getting high profits。
16. 参见第 5 段第 1 句。
17. 参见第 5 段第 2 句冒号后面的内容。
18. 参见第 5 段最后 1 句 as 后面的内容。
19. 参见第 6 段第 1 句。
20. 参见第 6 段第 2 句及其后面的内容。
21. 参见第 7 段第 2 句及其后面的内容：navigating bureaucratic waters and a mastery of patent rules。
22. 参见第 7 段第 3 句。
23. 参见第 7 段最后一句冒号后面的内容。
24. 参见第 8 段，尤其是最后 1 句。
25. 参见第 8 段第 1 句。
26. 参见第 8 段第 3 句 by 后面的内容。
27. 参见第 8 段第 4 句。
28~29. 参见第 9 段。
30. 参见第 9 段最后 1 句。
31. 参见第 10 段第 1 句，第 11 段第 1 句。
32. 第 10 段第 2 句及以后的内容。
33. 参见第 11 段第 2 句及以后的内容。
34. 参见第 8 段。
35. 参见第 11 段第 3 句：small firms。
36. 参见第 12 段倒数第 2 句。

## Exercises

### I. Reading Comprehension

1. The problem of profits in the USA is the corrosive lack of competition.
2. The profitable American firms park their profits abroad and abuse their monopoly positions or use lobbying to stifle competition.
3. a. The antitrust apparatus should be modernized by carefully examining the giant fund managers with crossholding, big tech platforms, mergers that lead to

high market share and too much pricing power and easing copyright and patent laws.

b. The life for startups and small firms should be made easier by recognizing bureaucracy as a problem.

4. F
5. F
6. B
7. navigating bureaucratic waters
8. have tried hard to keep rivals out by lobbying and mastering patent laws.

## II. Vocabulary Development

A.

1. The insurgencies of Donald Trump and Bernie Sanders
2. A naughty secret is a secret that cannot be made public but wayward and willful.
3. High profits.
4. To put/place/leave their profits/money abroad.
5. → Manipulate (to use something in a dishonest and harmful way).
   → Profits.
   → Stealing money from something such as a fund in small quantities over a period of time.
   → Substantial and factual.

B.
1. at  2. away  3. at  4. of  5. out

## III. From Reading to Speaking

Open.

## Reading Strategy

1. give up    2. talk loudly

## Reading 2

**Margin Questions**

1. 参见第1段第1句冒号后面的内容。
2. 参见第1段第1句such as 后面的内容。
3. 参见第2段第1句。
4. 参见第2段第2句。
5. 参见第2段第3句。
6. 参见第2段第3句 including 后面的内容。
7. 参见第4段第1句 as 后面的内容。
8. 参见第4段第2~3句。
9. 参见第5段内容。
10. 参见第5段第1句 at first 后面的内容。
11. 参见第5段最后一句 adding 后面的内容。
12. 参见第5段最后一句冒号后面的内容。
13. 参见第6段第2~4句。
14. 参见第7段第2句冒号后面的内容。
15. 参见第7段最后1句。

## Exercises

### I. Reading Comprehension

1. The social responsibilities for a company include workforce diversity, improving the environment, helping the poor in the community and a good relation with all stakeholders.
2. The company has been generous in

# Key to the Exercises

international grants and gifts in the communities, including earthquake relief in Turkey, community building projects in Japan, contributions for schools in China, school computers in Romania, special education in Malaysia and shore protection in France.

3. The corporate citizenship is evaluated with the in-house data, the data from KLD and the data about its relationship with the stakeholders.
4. Because they also make investments in companies.
5. To change what it means to be a good corporate citizenship and to move corporations toward ever-better practices in stakeholder relations.

## II. Vocabulary Development

A.
1. → A business journal
   → To trumpet/To focus on/To draw attention to
2. → They did things like earthquake relief in Turkey, community building projects in Japan, contributions for schools in China, school computers in Romania, special education in Malaysia and shore protection in France.
3. → To improve/To perfect
   → Stockholders is a part of stakeholders.
4. → Improprieties include scandals like misstated financial information, and antitrust conviction.

B.
1. to   2. into   3. of   4. to   5. As

## III. From Reading to Writing

Open.

## Reading 3

## Exercises

### I. Reading Comprehension

1. Peace; helping the poor
2. the micro-credit model
3. helping to create economic and social development from below
4. to eliminate poverty in the world
5. he got his PHD as a Fulbright scholar
6. the poor; women; economic growth and political democracy cannot be achieved unless people from below are developed

### II. Vocabulary Development

A.
1. Remove.
2. Property or something valuable promised to give to somebody if you cannot pay the money that you borrow/financial security.
3. Lending money to the poor without collateral; the poor.
4. Change.

B.
1. from   2. about   3. to
4. with   5. against

### III. From Reading to Speaking

Open.